Essential Clinical Care
for Sex Workers

Essential Clinical Care

for

Sex Workers

A Sex-Positive Handbook for Mental Health Practitioners

Theodore R. Burnes, PhD, MSEd, HSPP, LPCC
and Jamila M. Dawson, MA, LMFT

Foreword by Leya Tanit

North Atlantic Books
Huichin, unceded Ohlone land
aka Berkeley, California

Published by
North Atlantic Books
Huichin, unceded Ohlone land
aka Berkeley, California

Cover design by Jess Morphew
Book design by Happenstance-Type-O-Rama

Printed in the United States of America

Essential Clinical Care for Sex Workers: A Sex-Positive Handbook for Mental Health Practitioners is sponsored and published by North Atlantic Books, an educational nonprofit based in the unceded Ohlone land Huichin (*aka* Berkeley, CA) that collaborates with partners to develop cross-cultural perspectives; nurture holistic views of art, science, the humanities, and healing; and seed personal and global transformation by publishing work on the relationship of body, spirit, and nature.

North Atlantic Books' publications are distributed to the US trade and internationally by Penguin Random House Publishers Services. For further information, visit our website at www.northatlantic books.com.

Library of Congress Cataloging-in-Publication Data

Names: Burnes, Theodore R., author. | Dawson, Jamila M., author.
Title: Essential clinical care for sex workers : a sex-positive handbook
    for mental health practitioners / Theodore R. Burnes and Jamila M.
    Dawson.
Description: Huichin, unceded Ohlone land aka Berkeley, California : North
    Atlantic Books, [2022] | Includes bibliographical references and index.
Identifiers: LCCN 2022015625 (print) | LCCN 2022015626 (ebook) | ISBN
    9781623176808 (trade paperback) | ISBN 9781623176815 (ebook)
Subjects: LCSH: Sex workers—Mental health. | Sex workers—Mental health
    services. | Prostitution—Psychological aspects.
Classification: LCC RC451.4.S49 B87 2022 (print) | LCC RC451.4.S49
    (ebook) | DDC 306.7401/9—dc23/eng/20220831
LC record available at https://lccn.loc.gov/2022015625
LC ebook record available at https://lccn.loc.gov/2022015626

1 2 3 4 5 6 7 8 9 KPC 28 27 26 25 24 23

This book includes recycled material and material from well-managed forests. North Atlantic Books is committed to the protection of our environment. We print on recycled paper whenever possible and partner with printers who strive to use environmentally responsible practices.

Contents

Acknowledgments

Theo's Acknowledgments

This book has been a long time coming, a collection of thoughts for many years; thus, there are many people who have had an imprint on this work to whom I am ever grateful. Jamila Dawson, I am thankful beyond words for your laughter, your amazing knowledge about our field, your ability to help me reconnect with my voice and trust my intuition, and your bravery to say the things that need to be said. I am forever grateful for this journey with you! To our amazing consultants Angela, Vanessa, Sinnamon, and Jasmine: your stories, time, heart, and energy are some of the key ingredients of this project, and your feedback, openness, and authenticity have meant so much to this process. Your words have been with me every time I've written—so thankful to you for being a part of this journey. To Shayna Keyles and everyone at North Atlantic Books who believed in this project from the first day and provided nonstop encouragement: we have felt your support and are so excited for this work to be in the world!

To so many sex workers in professional and personal circles (current and previous), whose spirit, bravery, experiences, struggles, and successes have shaped my clinical work and this text. It continues to be an honor to witness your voices and journeys in this life experience, and I thank you. I thank you. I thank you.

To the clinicians in the field—my past, present, and future colleagues, acquaintances, supervisees, and friends whose experiences shine a light on knowledge that needs to be expanded and shared—thank you. A huge thank-you to the sex-worker-positive clinicians, from students in their first term of an academic practicum to seasoned clinicians contemplating retirement: I hope that this book accurately reflects your struggles, successes, and care of your clients. I also hope that the chapters in this book excite, enrich, inspire, and challenge you to provide even better mental health care.

Finally, to so many people who provided boundless support throughout the creation of this volume. To my partner and housemate, Craig Bauer, who continues to reflect love, compassion, and laughter into my world and for whom I am ever grateful. To my "frolleagues" (friends + colleagues), whose unending laughter, support, and consultation provide sustainability, accountability, and fun: Jeanne Stanley, Sylvie Taylor, Gregor Sarkisian, Tali Catz, Sarah Marvin, Daniel Walinsky, Anneliese Singh, Rachel Fusco, Alexis Arczynski, and Kenneth Edwards (among so many others)—thank you thank you thank you!!

Jamila's Acknowledgments

First and always, I honor my ancestors whose lives and dreams made my own possible.

Theo Burnes, writing this book has been more exciting than I could ever have expected and a process that I will forever be thankful for. It's one thing to be friends and colleagues with someone but it's quite another to join together to create something while navigating the vagaries of life (during a pandemic!) and *maintain* that deeply cherished friendship: Theo, we did it!! Thank you for being an incredible friend and a magnificent partner in this project. To Shayna Keyles, thank you for the encouragement and support that helped us hold to our vision, and to everyone at North Atlantic Books for making this book possible.

To our consultants, Sinnamon, Jasmine, Vanessa, and Angela, it's meant more than I can express to have your thoughts and experiences woven through the book. One of the very best parts of this process was the opportunity to talk and share time together. Each interview echoed for days in my head and informed and shifted my thinking as a person and clinician. The mutual care and exchange of ideas and experiences were truly a privilege and a deep pleasure. Thank you! Thank you! Thank you!

To the clients, students, supervisees, and colleagues at the Relational Center and beyond whom I've connected with over the years: Thank you for trusting me and being in the process of change-making with me.

To Mom, Dad, Khalid, and Martha, thank you for all the excitement, gentle encouragement, and pride you show in me, my career, and the way that I move through the world. Truly, the best of me springs from the seeds of integrity, justice, education, and imagination that weave through our family lines.

To Elre and Phi, my chosen family, thank you for being there for all my frustrated grumblings, for when I ramble on working out new ideas, for being excited for my wins, for being there when my burdens are too heavy, for spa days and movie nights, and for being you.

And, to Mistress Velvet.

Foreword

BY LEYA TANIT
FOUNDER, PINEAPPLE SUPPORT

IN JANUARY 2018, I left my home in Spain to fly to the XBIZ Awards in Los Angeles. I'd been a performer in the industry for many years, and before that, as a dancer in strip clubs. Over the years, I had found a home in communities of sex and sexuality, not just adult but also the world of BDSM and fetish.

Prior to the trip, I had taken some time off to deal with family issues, and my trip to the XBIZ Awards was going to be a comeback tour of sorts. I was beyond excited for it. Little did I know how that trip would change my life.

The show itself was a homecoming. I saw old friends, met new ones, and began the process of reestablishing myself as an active member of the adult community. But there was a pall over the show that year—in the past two months, more than five women in the industry had died after struggling with depression or addiction. During the awards ceremony, at least two nominees were unmistakably absent.

At what should have been the most exciting night of the year, many at the show were struggling to deal with their grief or rage. People spoke out, in some cases angrily from the stage, looking for someone or something to blame. I was shocked and devastated. Was something going on in the adult industry?

The mainstream media certainly thought so—or thought the claim would at least get clicks. From the first deaths, they blamed the victims, and blamed the work they did. They resorted to a well-worn playbook, portraying the women as broken and degraded, and the community around them as exploitative and uncaring. After all, the stories seemed to read: Who wouldn't kill themselves after working in such a disgraceful industry?

In conversation after conversation, online and onstage, there was outcry. Where are the services? Who could performers in need—including those struggling with grief today—turn to? The options were shockingly few. In addition to traditional issues in accessing mental health care, like financial concerns and stigma about going to therapy, there was a larger issue.

Many were scrambling. Some proposed working with mainstream organizations to train them to deal with sex workers. Others shared lists of therapists who were familiar with sex-worker issues. Others offered their own ears or couches for support. In public and private comments, people called for better mental health services, but no one seemed sure where to start.

We are a small and compassionate industry. We like to think we take care of our own because the outside world won't. Although there wasn't an easy solution, I was heartened to see both individuals and companies standing together, trying to grapple with personal grief and collective action. But I couldn't stop asking myself how this could have been avoided.

Although no one seemed to agree on the mechanism by which it would be done, the solution seemed clear—someone or something needed to provide easy access to therapy and mental health support for sex workers in the adult industry. Many in the industry are young people running their own small businesses. They manage shoots and sell clips or perform on cams. They have the least amount of health care and fewest tools for dealing with trauma. And, in the United States, even if you have health insurance, it likely doesn't cover therapy or recovery.

But access wasn't enough. Even when they can get services, sex workers have to deal with discrimination from therapists themselves. Too many therapists assume sex workers are damaged from their work, or that the solution to their mental health issues is to stop sex work altogether. Going to a therapist who is not sex-worker-aware can be traumatizing on its own.

As I flew back home to Spain, I was angry, but I felt a sense of responsibility to do something about this. Like many people, sex workers or not, I had struggled with depression, anxiety, and other issues. Not only was I lucky enough to benefit from work with a regular therapist, but my involvement in the sex industry and BDSM community had helped, not hurt me.

I arrived home and immediately took stock of my skills, background, contacts, and experience to see how I could help. Within a month, I'd drafted an initial blueprint for what mental health services could look like in the adult industry and how an organization could provide these services. I was excited, but also scared. I'd come back to the industry to reignite my career and earn money. Now, I was looking at a project that was vast and unfunded. But I knew something had to be done.

On April 6, 2018, I launched Pineapple Support. Our goal was simple: mental health support for all industry performers, without discrimination, judgment, or stigma.

In the BDSM community, the word *pineapple* is often used as a safe word, allowing performers to stop at any time. This small word is an incredibly powerful tool that helps to create a safe and comfortable space for everyone involved, and I wanted Pineapple Support to be a safe word for performers. Something they could say when the scene—well, life—got too much.

Raising funds was a challenge initially, with larger companies hesitant to provide support. I cleared out most of my savings to cover the creation of the organization, as well as the first couple of therapy sessions for performers, but the costs were racking up quickly.

Lifelines first appeared in the form of small donations from generous individuals, performers, and friends, with many more supporting us with advice, introductions, and moral encouragement. Some therapists even offered their services, free of charge, to people in crisis. I began looking for partners who might provide training for what's known as "active listening"—someone to talk to when things seemed overwhelming.

A small number of companies within the industry started to see what we were doing and began offering support. I'm so grateful to those who came aboard early. Their endorsement of what we were doing helped give us the momentum to attract others. By February 2019, Pineapple Support was granted 501(c)(3) status, and more and more established companies, brands, and organizations were rallying behind our mission.

It's now been four years since we started Pineapple Support, and in those years we've provided services for more than five thousand workers in the adult industry. We've connected performers with free and low-cost, one-on-one therapy, we've run support groups, and we've held workshops and summits. We've worked with individual performers and large, global companies.

And in that process, I've learned so much about both the issues and the solutions.

Almost everyone agrees that sex workers face greater mental health challenges than the civilian population—particularly depression and anxiety—but the reasons given for that are divisive. Traditionally, the mental health industry (and the larger society) believed that sex workers would engage in sex work only if they were damaged already—what some refer to as the "broken doll" theory. After all, what well-adjusted person would engage in sex work?

Of course, people engage in sex work for many reasons, from survival to financial stability to self-fulfillment. Some have traumatic experiences in their past, and some do not. And I've spoken with many people with mental health issues who gravitated toward the sex industry because it offered the space and flexibility to deal with those issues in a way a nine-to-five job does not. Others have come to exorcise trauma, or to reclaim their sexuality. And, of course, many come simply to explore their sexuality.

Unfortunately, our cultural disdain for sex work and the Hollywood stereotype of sex workers have never recognized the nuances of sex work. After all, the media rarely reports on happy, well-adjusted sex workers. Even in positive profiles, you can feel them digging to find a reason, a flaw, that's compelled them to this industry.

Over the four years since we started Pineapple Support, I've realized this stigma—both culturally and within the medical profession—is as deadly as anything in a sex worker's past. Although we've seen a gradual increase in awareness among therapists that sex work is real work, we're still constantly fighting myths. Here are some of the big ones:

Myth: Sex work is trauma. Too many therapists assume that sex work itself is traumatic, or the cause of mental illness. Although experiences in sex work can be traumatic, as experiences can be in other types of work, sex work itself is not inherently traumatic. When therapists look for trauma in consensual, sane, and safe sex work, it can be incredibly frustrating for sex workers seeking treatment.

Myth: Sex work is the result of trauma. One of the most common myths we face is the idea that sex workers are engaged in sex work because of some original trauma—usually assumed to be molestation, assault, abuse, or rape. Although these issues might be an issue for a sex worker, as they might be for anyone anywhere, it's patronizing and offensive to assume that the only reason someone is involved in sex work is to process trauma. For those who *are* processing sexual trauma, sex work can sometimes be a way to work through it.

Myth: Sex workers are trying to leave sex work. Some people in the sex industry see it as a temporary income stream, and hope to move into civilian life, but that doesn't mean everyone is. Therapists often assume that those in the industry are trying to get out, rather than seeing sex work as a viable—and often, in comparison to other options, preferable—way of funding their lives.

Myth: Sex work only leads to unhappiness. This is a type of victim-blaming that we see across the culture. Rather than acknowledging that the intense stigma around sex work—estrangement from family and friends, whorephobia in culture, discrimination, policing, social marginalization—causes unhappiness, some blame it on the work itself. These same tropes were once used as an argument against LGBTQ+ people in therapy, and were just as harmful.

We need therapists to understand that sex work can be empowering, and can provide an environment where people can thrive. If we're to solve the problem, we need stigma-free, sex-positive, kink-aware, sex-work-aware, LGBTQ+ friendly therapists. But unfortunately, these are in short supply. For most medical schools and therapy programs, sex workers just aren't a priority. Many therapists *want* to know how to help, but don't know where to start.

That's why *Essential Clinical Care for Sex Workers* is such a crucial tool in this fight. Over the years, I've gotten to know Jamila Dawson well, and my respect for her work and approach is enormous. *Essential Clinical Care for Sex Workers* lays out the issues, breaks down the stereotypes, and provides clear guidance for therapists dealing with sex workers.

My hope is that this book becomes essential reading for therapists, and a foundational text for the sex-worker-aware therapy movement. This is the book we've needed for a long time, and I couldn't be happier that it's finally here.

How to Use This Book

WE WROTE THIS BOOK as a guide to help the curious, willing, and committed clinician to more effectively support clients who are (or were formerly) sex workers. We've attempted to create a book that not only gives information and guidance about what to do with a client when you're in session, but also helps you to expand your own understandings about sexuality and sex work, even before you engage in a clinical relationship, or repair and refine the work that you're already doing.

We've designed this book to be read all the way through from beginning to end. However, although some chapters will refer to information from other chapters, every chapter can stand on its own. So if you're seeking support for a specific topic, we encourage you to flip to the chapter that relates most closely to your clinical needs. At the end of chapters 4, 5, and 7, there are assessments and templates for you to adapt and use in your practice.

As workshop presenters, supervisors, and clinicians, both of us appreciate the power of stories as a learning tool and, even more so, we deeply value the profound worth of lived experience. Because of this, beginning with chapter 1 and continuing throughout the book, we have included vignettes that are composites of professional or personal experiences that one or the other of us have had. Additionally, we were honored to secure interviews with four consultants for this project who currently do, or have done, sex work. It is extremely important to remember that there is no singular experience of sex work. The vignettes and the consultants' stories do not even begin to scratch the surface of the many variations that you will see when working with clients in the sex industry. What we've aimed to do with these vignettes is to give you elements to thoughtfully consider as you engage with your clients. With such considerations in mind, we have also selected excerpts from each of the consultants' interviews to provide an anchor to the main concept of each chapter. We hope that their experiences and observations challenge you to embrace one of the great paradoxes of clinical work: to notice the larger themes and patterns that envelop and shape our clients' lives while holding their multifaceted individuality in view. We're excited that you're engaging with this work!

1

INTRODUCTION

"It just doesn't work for me."

"I don't think therapy is a good idea for people like me."

"Let me tell you about my last psychologist. This man asked me what happened to me as a child that made me want to become a 'prostitute.' The minute he said the 'p' word, I told him that this wouldn't work. And I left."

"Are you kidding? I would never go to counseling."

"Oh, no way. I had to go to acupuncture to process how bad my last therapist was."

"This one social worker I worked with asked me to tell her about being a sex worker. For two sessions, I kept telling her things. She kept asking me questions about words. She asked me to define things. I kept responding. And then I realized, I was paying her to teach her. I didn't go back."

"If I want to feel bad about myself, I don't need to pay a therapist. I can hang out with people for free who can make me feel bad."

THE SEVEN RESPONSES ABOVE are just a small example of responses that we have heard in the last fifteen years. These responses come from a sample of sex workers who were asked about their experiences seeking therapy. These sex workers had spoken with mental health professionals in multiple disciplines, such as psychology, social work, marriage and family therapy, and counseling. They were seen in a variety of settings, such as clinics and private offices. What is unfortunate is that, despite the diversity of disciplines and settings, the answers were often similar. Many people who work in the sex industry have a strong aversion to going to therapy. Or, if they try therapy, they do not stay long.

How have we heard these responses? We are two licensed clinicians in the western United States. We have worked in community mental health agencies, private practice offices, hospitals, and university counseling centers. We have worked with clients of many races, ethnicities, genders, and sexual orientations. We are two licensed supervisors and educators in mental health training programs. Jamila is a licensed therapist and a sex educator. As a sex educator in various settings (sex stores, classrooms, workshops, trainings, conferences, and many other settings), Jamila began to notice the discomfort of many mental health providers in various disciplines in talking about sex work. She noticed clinical supervisors of pre-licensed therapists who were accruing the necessary training and experience who moved away from talking about sex work when they were reviewing supervisees' cases. She also noticed that many providers had no ability to talk about sex work when writing treatment plans, case conceptualizations, or referral notes. In addition, Jamila would also see clients in her clinical practice. She would continuously see clients in the sex industry who would tell her about their experiences in therapy.

Like Jamila, Theo has been seeing clients and working inside and outside academia facilitating courses, workshops, and in-service trainings about sexuality and therapy. He would simultaneously and continuously provide mental health services to clients in the sex industry who would tell him about their previous experiences in therapy. Most of these experiences were negative, resulting in Theo apologizing on behalf of his profession, hoping that things would get better. In his work as a supervisor, Theo would also hear from supervisees about how their former supervisors would actively avoid the topic of sex work. Over his career, Theo also conducted several studies about the resilience and agency of communities of sex workers, including their social support, their care for each other, and their ability to adapt to adverse working environments. Over and over again in his community-based research with sex workers, Theo heard of the horrible experiences of sex workers who were clients in therapy and counseling.

As our lives began to intersect, our vision of the problem (and possible solutions) became clearer. As we began to work with one another—first in a community mental health setting, next in a private practice setting as office mates, and then later in a university setting—we noticed patterns in what our clients and students were telling us. We noticed the same discomfort over and over again. As we both began doing advocacy work in sex-worker-led organizations and on behalf of sex workers' rights groups, we continued to hear the same concerns about access to and sustainability of mental health services for individuals working in the sex industry.

As mental health professionals, we have worked with young adults, adults in their midlife, and older adults. We have worked with other therapists as consultants, colleagues, and supervisors. We have used a variety of theoretical orientations, manualized treatments, and best practices. And, in all of these different constellations of mental health treatments, the responses that open this chapter are still the most common. Throughout our working relationship as colleagues and sex-positive mental health professionals, we would proclaim to each other, "There needs to be more training! There needs to be a book!" We would stand outside of our university, talking late into the night. We would meet for meals and coffee, and our conversation would inevitably turn to the need for this book. And then we got the opportunity to write the book that so many of our clients told us that our colleagues needed. That *we* needed. That we all needed—to heal and to do better.

Despite the fact that many individuals in the sex industry face the same obstacles in their lives that many of us do, there are data to suggest that sex workers utilize mental health services at lower rates than their peers in other industries and occupations.[1] So, why is the incidence of sex workers who participate in therapy so low? The reason is not because sex workers don't need support. Indeed, the need for sex workers to have supportive mental health services is crucial, as many sex workers engage in work environments that can involve harassment, violence, and danger.[2] In fact, the discrimination and harsh work environments that many sex workers experience often necessitate such support.[3] Further, the cumulative impact of a needed job that receives systemic hatred creates an inequality that undoubtedly results in workers' struggles with mental health.[4]

What becomes clearer after reviewing the data is that many mental health providers do not have competence in providing services for this specific population accessing treatment. Such framing of this problem is gaining increasing traction in a variety of mental health disciplines, including psychology, social work, marriage and family therapy, professional counseling, and psychiatric nursing.[5] Further, such a dynamic is not specific to mental health care, as different health care disciplines outside of mental health care also struggle with their clinicians' lack of competence in providing comprehensive health care to people in the sex industry.[6]

What Is Sex Work?

Before we keep investigating sex workers' participation in therapy, we want to stop and define who sex workers are. *Sex work* is broadly defined as the exchange of sex for money, other services, or goods.[7] Sex work has been traditionally stereotyped as referring only to street-based work. However, sex workers are a diverse group, and sex work takes many forms. Thus, this career expands upon street work and also encompasses a variety of occupations, including (but not limited to) live camming/online sex work, creating adult content through a subscription site, sugaring/being a sugar baby, exotic dancing/stripping, performing in adult movies, facilitating phone sex, and providing home/hotel service. Sex workers also include escorts, professional dominants or submissives, massage parlor employees, brothel employees, and fetish performers. These forms can be grouped into two major subtypes, defined as "direct" (direct contact with another person) and "indirect" (sex work that takes place from afar) providers. Further, these two subtypes can be further distinguished by clientele, income, risk, gender identity, and location.[8] We will discuss more about these differences in roles in chapter 2.

With all of these different examples of various types of sex work, questions begin to surface about the number of people who work in the sex industry within the United States. Many researchers have noted the difficulty of ascertaining specific numbers of people in the sex industry, in part due to the stigma of sex workers' self-identifying their occupation or career for research purposes.[9] Specifically, there are few data about the demographics or statistics for sex workers as an occupation in the United States.[10] Despite the lack of these data, numerous theoretical writings have noted that sex work transcends many dimensions of individual and cultural diversity. Sex workers identify with many ages, genders, and sexual orientations. They come from all parts of the globe, and reflect different ethnicities, races, nationalities, and cultural groups. They endorse many different ability statuses, diagnoses, and health conditions. Thus, the term *sex worker* refers to a large and very heterogeneous group of individuals.

Privilege and Power

As we consider who sex workers are, we also need to explore how their intersecting identities create added experiences of oppression and marginalization for some of them—which is a primary theme throughout this book. In providing this context, we also think it's important to introduce a few key themes that will reoccur throughout our writing. In short, we can't understand mental health services with sex workers if we can't understand privilege, oppression, and marginalization. Although we will discuss more about the different dimensions and labor of sex work in the next chapter, understanding the context in which sex work is embedded is a critical aspect of understanding the sex industry. At times, a sex worker's identity will intersect with other aspects of their personhood and identity. Sometimes, parts of a sex worker's identity are favored in the environments in which they live, work, or engage. Individuals with these systemically selected identities receive unearned advantages based on these identities. *Privilege,* or *cultural privilege,* is a system of advantage based on someone's identification with a cultural majority group.[11]

Privilege impacts multiple aspects of a sex worker's life, such as race, gender, and social class. For example, Jordan, a twenty-year-old, African

American, cisgender, gay male sex worker living in Melbourne, Australia, may have gender identity privilege (systemic, structural advantages based on his being cisgender) and male privilege (systemic, structural advantages based on his being male) because both of these identities make him part of a group that receives many advantages solely based on their sex and their gender identity. However, he may also lose other advantages because of his racial identity and gay male identity, which are not seen as having privilege in his environment. Jordan's intersecting identities exemplify how each sex worker is a unique combination of both privileged and oppressed identities.

Cultural privilege affects sex work primarily through a lens of power. *Power* refers to an individual's capacity or ability to direct or influence the behavior of others or the course of events. Employers or clients with power might use their privilege as a form of power to have sex workers act or do something in a particular way.[12] For example, Jordan (described in the paragraph above) may suggest or engage in a certain type of sexual behavior with his client, Tyler, and he may assume that Tyler will make his own decisions about these behaviors and speak up if he does not wish to participate in them. However, if we know that Jordan is an African American, cisgender, gay male, and Tyler is a White, cisgender, bisexual male, we understand that the dynamic in this exchange of sex for money may have a component of cultural privilege. Specifically, given Tyler's White and male cultural privilege in this sex-work transaction, Tyler may assume that he can ask for certain sexual acts or certain high-risk sexual behaviors, whereas Jordan may not feel comfortable saying no to these sexual practices or feel that he is able to do so because of the oppression that he has experienced. Members of the sex-work economy need to explicitly discuss such dynamics of privilege and power in the context of sex work, but often do not.[13] As the negotiation of power is an inherent part of sex work, we will explicitly address and discuss these issues in all chapters of this book.

Marginalization and Oppression

When a variety of individuals, such as global leaders, legislators, directors of mental health organizations, and health care providers, use their cultural privilege and power to separate sex workers from resources, they are engaging in marginalization.[14] Marginalization can also occur in the form of *unconscious bias,* or biases that people do not know that they have about sex workers. Unconscious bias often influences our behaviors in ways that we do not realize—particularly in behaviors related to the world of vocation and work.[15] We, or people close to us, may engage in marginalization regarding sex work based on these unconscious biases. For example, a colleague of yours may use insulting or denigrating language to describe sex workers' process and work. In another example, sex workers can be marginalized by not having their identities reflected in research studies, as many researchers predominantly sample certain sex workers (mostly White, cisgender women who perform certain kinds of sex work). You'll learn more about this research bias in chapter 3.

Marginalization in sex work is not a new phenomenon; in fact, many historical and contemporary analyses have documented that it has happened at different points in history at larger, systemic levels. For example, political scientist Sonu Bedi wrote about the term *sexual racism,* which this author defined as "prioritizing an individual as a possible romantic, intimate partner on account of their race in a way that reinforces extant racial hierarchy or stereotypes."[16] Sexual racism is not only about the individual choices made when selecting romantic partners; in fact, it's a way that systems of oppression shape an individual's partner choices.[17] When sexual racism is specifically applied to sex work, sociologist Angela Jones wrote about how it thwarts the success of Black-identified women, particularly in the camming field, because race and nationality play a pivotal role in the monetary success of webcam models. Jones explicitly noted that bodies of color have lower sexual capital.[18] This example shows how the combination of prejudice, racist behaviors, and the power structures of White privilege applies directly to sex work.

Marginalization is related to but different from *oppression,* a form of injustice that occurs when an entire social group is subordinated while another is privileged.[19] Oppression often happens at a group, community, or organizational level, which will result in people individually experiencing the result of oppression. Examples of systemic oppression felt by sex workers at an individual level include stigma, access to health care, legislation, and safety. Oppression is maintained, not always deliberately, by a variety of different mechanisms, including social norms, stereotypes, institutional rules, implicit biases, and stereotypes.[20] As with marginalization, oppression carries over into sex work as well. For example, White actors in pornographic films are overrepresented in comparison to actors of color in porn films, and scholars find that producers of these films often pay female-identifying performers less than male-identifying performers.[21, 22]

These examples of systemic racial oppression can lead to White supremacy, a particular type of oppression in cultural, economic, and political systems that sustain White people's dominance over almost all sectors of society. Through White privilege and White supremacy, individuals create explicit and implicit false ideas through everyday dynamics in a wide variety of social settings about the dominance of White people.[23] We can again connect these false ideas to elements of sex work. For example, lack of awareness about White supremacy may cause some of us to unnecessarily eroticize or fetishize certain sex workers of color or transgender-identified sex workers, creating false stereotypes about certain sex workers' jobs and work process.

When we locate the topic of sex work within concepts such as marginalization and oppression, we see how mental health service providers may see information at only a micro, individual level. Given that many providers work only in individual or community settings, they often provide only direct services (like individual, relational, family, and/or group therapy), and so they think about peer-to-peer interactions as the main application for marginalization and oppression. As providers, we think about the bias and discrimination that happens in our work and in our therapy room. However, we often do not think in larger, more structural ways. We do not think about the various ways that marginalization and oppression create systems that disadvantage sex workers. One example includes the ways that oppression impacts larger structural bodies, such as the different ways that law enforcement officials may interact with Black sex workers in comparison to White sex workers. Another example includes how bias translates into a lack of access to a variety of social services, such as legal protections and medical care.

When asking the question *"Who are sex workers?"* we also have to ask, *"What oppressive systems have sex workers been forced to fight? How have sex workers internalized these oppressive systems?"* We do not think about how these systems create unique stressors for sex workers, because we are so focused on the clients in front of us and therefore focus only on our individual interactions. This focus on micro-level interactions without focusing on meso- and macro-level interactions can result in an erasure of contextual factors. Sex workers feel this erasure when they walk into our offices, email our clinics, and call our helplines. They feel this erasure when they look at our websites, see our social media posts, and fill out our surveys. This erasure is a key ingredient in further marginalization of individuals in the sex industry, and the reason why we have heard so many of the quotes at the beginning of this chapter.

You may have heard some of these terms before. Particularly if you are a therapist with a graduate degree, concepts such as oppression and marginalization are hopefully not new to you. However, we hope that this introductory discussion of these concepts in this book (which will be explored in many later parts of this volume) helps you to already consider the ways that marginalization and oppression compound the experiences of work-related stress for many sex workers. A series of concepts that, when continuously combined, many therapists may not even consider, much less explicitly notice and integrate into their clinical work. As you begin to see that sex work isn't just about sex, but also about work—including workplace climate, workplace harassment, and workplace discrimination—you may start to acknowledge just how needed a shift in clinical practice with sex workers actually is.

Intersectionality as Context

When we consider psychological services with sex workers, experiences of marginalization and oppression are of extreme importance. Many times, we may consider experiences of marginalization only one at a time—maybe based on race, or gender, or sexual orientation. However, for sex workers with multiple marginalized identities, clinical work addressing intersectionality is of extreme importance. According to labor rights activist Kimberlé Crenshaw,[24, 25] a critical race theorist, the concept of *intersectionality* means (1) for some people, different marginalized identities intersect in different ways, (2) the intersection of these marginalized identities may create unique experiences of marginalization, and (3) these unique intersections affect membership in larger communities or social groups. Crenshaw noted that these multiple, marginalized identities are not additive (that is, we do not stack these marginalized identities on top of one another and claim that the person among us with the most marginalized identities is the most oppressed). Rather, Crenshaw noted that these identities are intersecting and are therefore critical in shaping an individual's experiences.[26] Other scholars[27, 28] have expanded this definition to identify patterns of oppression and marginalization that are interrelated and utilize connections between identities of race, ethnicity, gender, ability, geographic origin, sexual orientation, gender identity, acculturation status, and age to create additional threats and more vulnerability to oppression for individuals with these multiple identities.

When combining these different definitions of intersectionality, we see the unique stress that multiple marginalized identities may have on sex workers. For example, suppose that Maria is a Puerto Rican American woman who has recently begun to work in the sex industry as a cam artist. As part of her entry into the work, Maria decides to access some different events in her local community to seek support. However, when she goes to a local event for sex workers, she unfortunately finds that most of the attendees are White, and she does not feel comfortable expressing her cultural and ethnic heritage at that event due to some of the attendees' racist comments. Maria feels unsupported and also has to deal with the impact of these racist comments. When Maria goes to another local event hosted by local members of her Puerto Rican community, she hears some comments that are marginalizing to people in the sex industry, leaving her feeling uncomfortable about different parts of who she is. Maria's experiences at these two events describe how the intersection of her identities as Puerto Rican and someone exploring her relationship to sex work makes her feel uncomfortable in multiple spaces.

Let's Not Talk about Sex

With this multifaceted view of sex work, it becomes apparent that education must be culturally and systemically comprehensive in order for us to understand the numerous aspects of sex work. In addition to power, marginalization, and privilege, what is also often left out of conversations about sex work and therapy is the lack of comfort that many clinicians have with sexuality in general. Specifically, many clinicians routinely divorce themselves from their own sexual experiences and neglect to understand that sexual well-being for all of us is part of a larger system of emotional and mental well-being. For many of us as therapists, sex feels "off limits," too taboo of a subject to bring into the therapy room. Historical understandings of sexuality within psychology, counseling, and marriage and family therapy have focused on sexuality as a problem in all of its forms. If you have too much sex, you have a problem—and if you have too little sex, you have a problem. In the "Goldilocks approach" to sexual well-being, you have to be just right—and just right is based on a very specific depiction of sexuality for a White, heterosexual, able-bodied person who experiences pleasure and sex only in socially acceptable manners, customs, and traditions. We know—this brings up a lot of sadness and anger for you. Us, too.

What's worse is that much of this way of thinking about sex (and, therefore, thinking about sex work) starts in graduate training programs for future therapists. A variety of studies of mental health training programs have found trends related to what is covered in their sexuality courses—models of diseases, some information about diversity in sexual orientations and genders, and a lot of information about diagnostic concerns related to sexual functioning.[29] Sometimes, there might be an elective class in sex therapy or human sexuality—but it's not required, and the students who often need to take the course are the ones who do not take it. Comprehensive human sexuality education for therapists-in-training often does not include information on sex work. Such education also does not include content on the comprehensive psychological, biological, emotional, labor rights, and sociological understanding of this unique profession.[30]

So, you may be asking, *"What about fieldwork and internships?"* These experiences often pair new, unlicensed therapists with a clinical supervisor to learn practical skills about doing therapy. Many scholars have studied whether therapists-in-training receive additional information about sexuality in practica and internships. The results are the same—therapists often receive the same training that problematizes sex.[31] Unfortunately, much of this training about synthesizing sexuality with one's mental health practice results in clinicians' harmful practices with people in the sex industry.

From this lack of sex education, therapists rarely explore how people may have internalized sex-negative attitudes and belief systems. *Sex-negative* actions are those that understand, relay, and/or depict sex as abnormal, wrong, or shameful. Examples include when we tell our friends that they "may have a problem" if they are interested in sex work, or when we watch a movie on Netflix that shows someone feeling shameful about their experience with sex work and think, "This character thinks that what they did is shameful, and it's in this movie, so it must be shameful." One kind of sex negativity, *erotophobia,* is a cultural or religious fear, disdain, disgust, or devaluing of sensual or sexual pleasure, the erotic capacities of the mind and body, and nonprocreative sexual practices.[32] Examples of erotophobia can include media messages that depict sexual desire as wrong, or government messages that insist the purpose of sex is for procreation only and not pleasure. Many scholars in sexuality studies have expanded upon this definition, including the point that erotophobia is actually an irrational reaction to the erotic, which in turn makes fearful individuals and society vulnerable to social control.[33]

In addition to the lack of education about sex work, of the multiple disciplines and frameworks on sexuality that influence how we train health care providers (specifically mental health care providers) about working with sex workers in a clinical setting, many of these frames do not take into account pleasure, trauma, and the sociopolitical systems that impact sex workers. However, one such framework *is* able to provide a practical means to understand and support sex workers and sexual wellness in general: sex positivity. *Sex positivity* is the integration of the physical, somatic, emotional, intellectual, social, and spiritual aspects of sex.[34] The World Health Organization (WHO) views human sexuality—including an individual's sexual intimacy, sexual identity, sexual orientation, and eroticism—as enhancing the individual's personality, communication, and relationships.[35] Sex positivity is also a term used to describe individuals and communities who emphasize openness, nonjudgmental attitudes, freedom, and liberation from anti-sex (pleasure-negative or sex-negative) attitudes.[36] Despite the advent of sex positivity in the literature, much of this framework has not yet been integrated into how clinicians are taught to address sexual topics (including sex work) in their work. The need for a text that uses sex positivity as a framework to address needed knowledge, attitudes, and skills to work with sex workers is at a critical high point.

A lack of sex education and the need for more sex positivity about sex work create another aspect of the rationale for this book. Within a dumping ground of erotophobia, clinicians are not talking about sex with their clients—either by actively refraining from it, or by making sex a problem when clients want to express it as a form of their own pleasure and joy. And when sex is a part of a client's job—a job that many of the client's family or friends consider immoral or wrong—the lack of discussion becomes a huge gap in the counseling or therapy process. It becomes difficult for a sex worker in therapy to continuously skip over details about their job to avoid offending their therapist. And so, many sex workers don't return to therapy—even if they have something else with which they need support. Thus, therapists have been taught neither about sexuality nor about sex work in particular, and now engage in unethical practices—at the expense of their clients' psychological functioning.

Why Is This Book Needed?

Theo: *Have there ever been mental health professionals that you have talked about your involvement in the sex industry with?*

Angela: *I think after I was here, in California, I started going to a mental health outpatient clinic. I had a therapist there who was connected to a substance abuse treatment center—she was a [marriage and family therapist]—and I did talk to her about my work.*

Theo: *Did you feel supported by that therapist?*

Angela: *No, she would always redirect me every time I wanted to bring it up, and I took the redirections as maybe judgment or dismissal. I would start to talk about sex work and she would redirect me to something else.*

Theo: *When did you start to recognize that? Did you ever have feelings about that process in the moment . . . or did you ever have feelings when it was happening?*

Angela: *When she was redirecting me? Absolutely. Yeah, it definitely made me feel disgusting, ashamed, sorry that I brought it up. It kind of reinforced the belief that I need to just compartmentalize my work and not understand it and not realize that this work was a part of me. I remember leaving those sessions feeling like it was something I need to hide.*

As is probably clear to you by this point, a comprehensive review of education in mental health training programs has demonstrated that clinicians are not being trained in working with the wide range of individuals involved in sex work.[37] As is noted in the conversation between Theo and Angela above, there is a need for a broad-based handbook that centers the diverse needs and experiences of individuals working in the sex industry with respect to mental health services. The need for clinicians-in-training in disciplines such as psychology, social work, marriage and family therapy, licensed professional clinical counseling, and substance abuse counseling (among others) to move from pathology-based sexual health models to sex-positive models that encourage sex worker well-being has received increasing attention by many professional organizations dedicated to human health and functioning (such as the World Health Organization[38]). However, specific attention to sex worker well-being approaches in the many mental health disciplines has continued to lag behind. Further, as human sexuality is often taught to clinicians using a White, western European paradigm that focuses on "normality," dysfunction, and STI/STD prevention and does not focus on sex as pleasurable, specific information about sex work is absent or problematized within mental health training programs.[39] The results are that, too often, sex workers are judged, problematized, traumatized, and infantilized by mental health providers and others.

What Will You Learn?

To meet the many needs that we have articulated about clinical practice with clients who are sex workers, this book will provide a variety of theoretical understandings, strategies, and interventions for mental health clinicians to provide better-quality therapy services for clients who are engaging in or who have engaged in sex work. This book holds that sex work is a funda-mentally legitimate occupation, and—due to stigma and criminalization—sex workers have particular needs and challenges concerning mental health.

Through engaging dialogue and reader-centered content, it is our hope that this volume will increase mental health therapists' self-awareness of their own relationship to sexuality, break down stereotypes, depatholo-gize sex work itself, and provide clear practices for the provision of quality psychotherapy. With this needed book, new and established clinicians will have a best-practice guide for treating clients who engage in sex work with dignity and respect while tending to the unique needs of this population.

In addition to our own experiences, we also invited four people to be consultants for this book. The conversation between Theo and Angela (one of our consultants) earlier in this chapter is just one of the many ways that these consultants have helped to shape the process and content in this volume that we are excited to share with you. Each of these consultants is either actively involved in sex work or has been involved in sex work histori-cally (or both). We want to make it clear that their experiences are their own and can illuminate aspects of sex work while simultaneously not describing all experiences and forms of sex work. We are honored and excited to share their words with you, and you can learn more about them and their work experiences, thoughts, and advocacy efforts at the end of our book. They not only reviewed our work and told us when we may have been leaving things out, but they also described experiences to us that were super helpful in framing and contextualizing the words that you're about to read.

This book has two main goals and objectives. The first is to increase mental health providers' awareness, knowledge, and skills for working with clients in the sex industry. The second is for therapists to challenge their own individual, collective, and systemic erotophobia and intersect-ing oppressions that are used to problematize sex work (and so many other things). In chapter 2, we will discuss types of sex work in more depth. We will provide an overview of current literature on the diversity of individuals who identify as sex workers and/or practice various types of sex work, in contrast with media portrayals of sex work. We'll also review problematic classification systems used in previous literature, classifying sex work by environment and practice location. We will end the chapter introducing the term *whorearchy* and identifying practical ways for clinicians to dismantle it in various domains of their professional practice. In this chapter, we will address underreporting of sex work related to stigma and address common myths rooted in erotophobia.

In chapter 3, we will ask, "How did we get here?" Specifically, how have unchallenged historical understandings of sex work created problematic frameworks in which providers engage? We will introduce the oppressive paradigm[40] in mental health research and training about sex workers and how this paradigm has impacted various domains of clinical work. We will also review problematic reporting processes related to sex workers (including research bias, inappropriate generalizability, etc.); the lack of systematic inclusion related to issues of power, privilege, and oppression throughout mental health work with sex workers; and the absence of clinical training and practice for those working in topics of sexuality.

In chapter 4, we will shift from theoretical and macro understandings to a more micro lens of how these understandings can be shifted in clinical practice by looking at a self-examination of your own attitudes toward sex work. We will review ethics literature in mental health on the need for self-awareness and self-examination for clinicians. We'll also discuss clinicians' acknowledging and reducing of their internal biases; areas of continuing education (including Sexual Attitude Reassessments, or SARs); consultation/supervision when needed; and creation of clinically sex-positive/whore-positive spaces.

In the second half of the book, we will shift more from theory to practice. In chapter 5, we will begin to discuss best clinical practices in the beginning stages of treatment with clients who are sex workers. In this chapter, we will dive into information about the initial assessment process and how to build rapport during initial phases of treatment with clients. We will also highlight findings regarding harmful attitudes and practices among service providers. Through discussions and specific examples, we will describe to you the process of finding or seeking referrals, practices and stances to avoid, and the indicators that reduce barriers and help lead sex workers to contact a mental health provider.

In chapters 6 and 7, you will learn that, too often when working with this population, clinicians may choose a one-size-fits-all approach or approaches that are individualistic and locate the client's distress as a personal failing. We will discuss different theories and why they are and are not useful for this population as well as ways to increase the client's support network and increase their sense of agency. We will review different ways of understanding case conceptualization and mental health interventions that you can construct in order to help with the ongoing treatment process. We will also identify specific areas that need to be incorporated with care and humility, as well as certain questions to avoid asking. In chapter 7, we will address the ongoing need to tend to the clinician-client relationship, navigating safety concerns within a frame of mutual growth, and utilizing a "power-with" not "power-over" frame of navigating the course of treatment. We will discuss establishing rapport, building relationship (trust is built; it is never a one-time event), ensuring safety, satisfying mandated reporting, balancing power differentials, sustaining patience and adaptability, maintaining the therapeutic alliance, recognizing potential pitfalls, repairing inevitable ruptures, making room for the unexpected, and addressing termination: endings and beginnings.

We hope that this introductory chapter has helped you locate the need for this book. We hope that you have a better understanding of the state of mental health services with a group of people who represent diverse identities, experiences, and scopes of work. This group of people also are focal points of larger systems of power and structures of oppression and inequality. Clinical practice with sex workers also reflects lots of erotophobia, lack of training about sex, and our own discomfort with the topic. Our clients who are sex workers need us to be better. We have our work cut out for us. Without any more time to waste, let's get started.

2

TYPES OF SEX WORK

With a number of other therapists, I have not been open about sex work, or I've been selective. I think a lot of people probably tell their therapist some sort of sliver version of the big picture. The stigma is very clear. It is very complete. It has a kind of Freudian damned if you do, damned if you don't capacity, if that makes sense. It's like, if you're smart, you're an exception; if you didn't go to school, it's because you're dumb. Right? Okay. So the stigma is a very, very complex, but very clear set of beliefs about who and what sex workers are in this culture. It has got its racism. It's got its classism, it's got its gender hierarchies, it's got all of these things in there. And so what that told me is that the stigma is the air we breathe. And that I simply cannot presume that any one person has done the work themselves to destigmatize sex work internally for themselves. And that means every single person that I talked to, I am gauging what level of anti-stigma work they've done in their life for themselves so that I can figure out what my level of safety is. One of the main problems that I see is, for me, and for other workers, we can't assume that the therapist we're talking to believes in sex work and healthy living as coexisting. So therapists have to have a model of emotional health. That includes sex work as a job; they have to see sex work as something you can do healthfully.

—VANESSA

NOW THAT WE HAVE shared with you the *why* of this book, we hope that we might go a little deeper into the *who*. Although we provided you with some definitions in chapter 1 about what sex work is, we want to also provide more context about *who sex workers are.* You read in chapter 1 that it is hard for several reasons to provide prevalence rates of sex workers within the industry. However, despite this difficulty, it is imperative that we review some of what we do know (or what we think we know), and examine some of the problems with how we see sex workers as people and as laborers. As alluded to above by our consultant Vanessa, we want to provide you with an overview on the diversity of individuals who identify as sex workers and/or practice sex work (i.e., types of sex workers) who may hope to work with you as a mental health provider. We also hope to contrast these trends in sex-worker communities with inaccurate media portrayals of sex work, as well as address some common myths about sex workers that are rooted in erotophobia. Additionally, we want to address the positional hierarchy that exists within sex work—the whorearchy—and how it relates to internalized and externalized systems of oppression.

Activist Carol Leigh coined the term *sex work* in 1978.[1] Leigh originally understood sex work as identifying specific jobs, including street work, strip work, parlor work, escort work, working independently, mistressing, peep show work, telephone work, and topless dancing.[2] Earlier literature in various mental health disciplines referred to sex workers as "prostitutes," "streetwalkers," and "hookers," terms that many sex-positive researchers found degrading and suggestive of a lack of agency in the work.[3] Scholars also noted that referencing women as "girls" (e.g., call girls) further undermined the agency of female-identified sex workers.[4] Unfortunately, these early labels and terms did not focus on sex workers as people, and sex work as an industry, but had strong roots in the hatred of sex, and the hatred of women. Mental health disciplines have come a bit further since these early discussions, but not much. We still have large problems in understanding who sex workers are through a lens of respect and sex positivity.

Who Are Sex Workers?

When defining the scope and practice of sex workers within a mental health context, we must have the ability to understand sex work itself. Specifically, we want to situate sex work within a labor rights orientation. *Sex work is work.* Rather than recognizing this, erotophobic systems have often made discourse about sex work gravitate to conversations about sex and morality (for more on these erotophobic systems, we refer you back to chapter 1). These conversations often happen without the input of sex workers about the work in which they engage. They often revolve around whether sex workers should or should not be involved in the work, as opposed to clinicians' dedication to meeting clients where they are and providing support to help them cope with their work-related stressors (we will discuss these themes of clinical practice in later chapters of the book).

Therapists are able to have these conversations about worker rights. When we as mental health workers serve clients who are unsupported or have less protection in their work (such as individuals in the cleaning service industry or independent contractors who work as musicians-for-hire), we often do not have conversations about the morality or judgment of their work. We instead hold space for these clients and find them support. In addition, we may also have conversations with these clients about labor, workplace climate, and workplace safety (including harassment and discrimination). These topics are often left out, erased, or altogether eliminated from clinical conversations or when sex workers interface with health care providers. By inviting you to imagine your clinical process differently, we also hope that you will initiate or support conversations about sex work and connect them to context about politics, total health for workers and employees, the economy, and migration.

From a labor rights framework, understandings of who identifies as a sex worker have come a long way, resulting in the list of many examples of different types of sex work that you reviewed in the previous chapter. These newer understandings of sex work, which many sex workers prefer, help to acknowledge the existence of agency and empowerment in the work. They also make room for conversations about unions that advocate for safety and equal rights for people in the sex-work industry. Whatever term your client uses to identify themselves, keep in mind that some older terms may be considered derogatory and should be used with caution. Also, technological advances have increasingly moved some sex work from the street to the internet, allowing sexuality to enter people's homes at higher rates and making the purchase of sex work more anonymous.

"Reel" but Not Reality

When trying to understand who sex workers are, we often do not take cultural variables into account. More specifically, in a variety of health care systems there is a lack of understanding that accurately describes the various characteristics of sex workers around the globe. Media depictions of sex workers often present sex workers as White, cisgender, able-bodied women who loosely fall into two specific categories. The movie reels of the 1950s through the reels of today are filled with inaccurate portrayals of individuals in the industry. One category is the "damsel sex worker" myth, or the myth that a sex worker has no resilience, is often cut off from all resources, has no agency, and cannot do anything to escape the "cruel world of sex work" until a male-identified person performs a "rescue." A second category is the "hopeless" myth, or the portrayal of a sex worker who is "beyond hope." In this second category, media portrays sex workers as addicted to drugs and alcohol with no hope of recovery, homeless with no hope of ever finding shelter, and also with no agency and no connection to resources. Analyses of media—specifically, motion pictures—have investigated these and other myths, noting that sex workers are not portrayed accurately. These misrepresentations often provide incomplete pictures, which can lead policymakers, government officials, and mental health workers to make mistakes in their work.[5] These inaccurate portrayals often completely erase the importance of labor rights within the group of workers.

These myths and inaccurate media representations leave out huge groups of sex workers. *Huge.* Large numbers of individuals involved in sex work are marginalized due to race, ethnicity, and/or gender identity compared with individuals in many other service industries.[6] For example, sex workers of various ability statuses often work with clients of equally varying ability statuses. This work may be not only about sex for money, but also about rehabilitation of one's sexuality and/or sexual self-efficacy after a traumatic brain injury and/or a traumatic event such as a car accident. For example, clients may engage with sex work for matters of healing traumatic sexual experiences or exploring various facets of sexual identities. Further, women of color (particularly African American–identified and Latinx-identified women) have been found to be disproportionately underrepresented in sex work.[7] These experiences of sex work are often erased from media. Further, cisgender-women-focused cultural biases can allow us to reject the notions that people of other sexes and genders (men, transgender women, and intersex women) can, and do, enter sex work.

One group of sex workers where myths lead to increasing discrimination and oppression is transgender-identified sex workers of color.[8] The National Transgender Discrimination Survey (NTDS) was completed by more than 6,400 transgender adults in the United States between 2008 and 2009. Survey data from the NTDS indicated that transgender people experience high levels of discrimination in every area of life, as well as high levels of poverty, unemployment, homelessness, negative interactions with police, incarceration, and violent victimization.[9] Because of these factors, many trans-identified people decide to enter the sex-work industry to earn money and try to decrease the impact that poverty can have on their lives. Trans-identified sex workers are the most at risk for violence and harassment in the United States. They are at an even higher risk for these factors if they are people of color. In fact, responses on the NTDS indicated that Black and Black Multiracial respondents had the highest rate of sex-industry participation overall (39.9 percent), followed by those who identified as Hispanic or Latino/a (33.2 percent).[10] Those who identified as "White only" had the lowest rate of participation at 6.3 percent. These data begin to tell us a more complex story about sex workers that is entangled with discrimination, oppression, and resilience.

Social Location and Work Environment of Sex Work

In addition to understanding terminology and hierarchies within sex-worker communities, all of us as clinicians need to understand how the social and physical location of sex workers' work helps to create (or eliminate) protective factors for them. For any of us, where we work can help or hinder our comfort and safety at work. For some of us, a familiar location for work brings with it comfort and safety. If we feel connected to the location of where we work, we may be more likely to have an increased knowledge of resources that are adjacent or connected to our work location. For those of us who work with difficult situations, it may also be helpful for us to feel connected to our work so that we can find outlets for help in cases of crisis or assaults.

Previous literature in the field of psychology has a documented history of glorifying a hierarchy within communities of sex workers.[11, 12] These different tiers of hierarchy, or *classes* within the hierarchy, are differentiated by location of services and number of clients in a given time period. In one of the earliest and most cited examples in sex-work literature, John Exner and colleagues[13] identified five classes of female sex workers. *Class I,* or the *upper class* of the profession, were escorts who usually worked with clients of upper-middle-class or upper-class backgrounds. *Class II,* referred to as the *middle class,* consisted of "in-house workers" who typically worked in an establishment on a commission basis. *Class III,* referred to as the *lower middle class,* were street-based sex workers whose fees and place of work fluctuated considerably. *Class IV* sex workers were known as "commuters," and were typically involved in sex work to supplement family income, working on the street and far away from their home. Finally, *Class V* consisted of a specific type of street-based sex worker, or "drugs-for-sex street-based sex workers,"[14] and were considered the *lower class* of the profession.

The Whorearchy

Analyses of these historical hierarchies have used structural formulations of sex work to understand them differently than the first researchers may have intended. Using concepts such as privilege and oppression (remember chapter 1), many current sex-positive scholars and activists have found problems with these classification systems. Using terms such as "Class I" or "lower middle class" is fraught with classist understandings of work and labor. Current activists and scholars have named these classification systems the *whorearchy,* or the hierarchical system by which people often rank sex workers from "elite" to "inferior."[15] Porn star and sex-worker advocate Belle Knox noted that the whorearchy is arranged according to intimacy of contact with clients and police: "The closer to both [clients and police] you are, the closer you are to the bottom. That puts 'outdoor' workers . . . at the foundation. They are disdained by 'indoor' prostitutes, who find clients online or via other third parties. They are disdained by the strippers and escorts who perform sex acts for clients, who are disdained by those who don't. At the top sit sex workers who have no direct contact with cops or clients, such as cam girls and phone sex operators."[16]

Unfortunately, sex workers also internalize these ranking systems, using the same system to classify themselves. This internalized whorearchy also connects with other forms of internalized oppression (such as internalized racism, colorism, sexism, homophobia, and classism, to name a few) to create intersecting matrices of harm and isolation. Using Crenshaw's model of intersectionality that you learned about in chapter 1, we can begin to see how these unique intersections can greatly impact a sex worker's resilience and self-esteem. This lack of resilience results in greater mental health symptoms (such as symptoms related to anxiety and depression) and also increased negative health-related behaviors, such as lack of self-care or increased use of drugs and/or alcohol. It's important for us to reemphasize: *These symptoms are not innate for sex workers; rather, they are the result of coping with their negative contexts and unsupportive environments.* Sex workers often internalize these oppressive classification systems and in turn use these systems to classify themselves and each other, and non–sex workers might also use these classifications unwittingly.[17, 18]

As our collective understandings of sex workers have thankfully continued to evolve, current literature defines "street-based sex workers" as those who conduct their work on the street.[19] "Indoor sex work" includes working as escorts, exotic dancers, telephone sex providers, brothel workers, independent contractors, peep show workers, parlor workers, crack den workers, dungeon workers, and massage parlor workers. Independent contractors involved in sex work recruit their clients in bars, in nightclubs, via the internet, or in print media.[20] They may also choose to work in their own homes or in the homes of their clients.

COVID-19 allowed many modifications to sex work, blurring the lines between what is "indoor" and "street-based" for many individuals for purposes of health and safety. Workers reported drive-through strip clubs, higher rates of telework (camming, posting online videos, pictures, etc.), and more fear of in-person work due to clients' possible lack of truthfulness about statuses related to vaccination and being immunocompromised.[21] Many migrant sex workers have had to put their health and safety at risk because they are excluded from accessing social and health services within the United States. Thus, many of these workers were not able to stay at home, physically distance, or stop work in order to survive.[22] COVID-19, in essence, has begun to blur the lines of a rigid, pre-pandemic whorearchy. We are excited to see these lines blurred, as they have been blurred so often for many sex workers already. How this blurring will shape the field of sex work remains to be seen.

So, does the whorearchy hold true in current understandings of sex work? Unfortunately, this whorearchy is still prevalent in much of the discourse about sex workers and among communities of sex workers. For example, many sex-positive researchers and activists have used the whorearchy in conversations about safety for sex workers. Specifically, they often identify escort work as having the highest status of sex work based on location.[23] Some consider the work of escorts to be safer,[24] more profitable,[25] and more discreet[26] than other forms of sex work. One factor regarding working conditions is whether escorts work independently or for an agency.[27] Independent sex workers have been found to be in the best relative position to determine their working conditions, including clientele, cost of labor, work pace, sexual activities performed while working, and net earnings.[28] Although independent escorts' work may provide more autonomy, independent sex-work contractors are not protected by labor codes or occupational health and safety regulations regarding employer responsibility.[29] These characteristics can help us to understand sex work through the lens of a labor rights movement. Who sex workers are cannot be separated from the work that they do . . . and how we view that work is a pivotal part of who we think sex workers are.

Implications of Location and Work Environment on Sex Workers' Well-Being

Obstacles stemming from the location of a person's job are not an uncommon topic for sex workers. However, these obstacles lead to the oppression that stems from biases and ill-thought-out legislation. When we look more in depth at the demographic characteristics of sex workers, it is important to note that different types of sex work are associated with different levels of support, stigma, resources, and safety. In addition to the location of a sex worker's labor, professional organization of sex work is an important facet of understanding protective factors for sex work. Management regulations significantly impact the work environment of off-street workers[30] and consequently make hierarchies more prevalent. For example, women who work in peep shows frequently have a glass barrier that separates them from their audience and have more control over the performer-client relationship (as opposed to dancers who work without a physical barrier). For peep show workers, management will discipline clientele, whereas exotic dancers depend on tips from customers and often are solely responsible for enforcing boundaries between legal and illegal touching.[31]

When analyzing the impact of location on sex workers' identities, we see that identification with certain types of sex work may result in more or less access to safety, resources, or social support (as noted by our consultant Vanessa in the beginning of this chapter). Access to resources, in turn, can also greatly impact the safety of these workers. For example, sex workers who have received sufficient education on STI prevention, who understand safe-sex practices, and who have access to regular STI screening (when compared to sex workers who do not have access to condoms or regular STI testing) often report greater experiences of agency in their work and are also more likely to access nonhealth resources (e.g., legal resources, housing resources). In-person sex workers who use websites to screen clients are also at a greater advantage when compared to escorts who do not have access to safety screening methods. Online sex workers, such as "cam girls" or professional adult film performers, are at a greater advantage compared to the safety risks and stigma associated with in-person sex work. The advantages to which online sex workers or adult film performers tend to have access are not because the work they do is inherently "better" than in-person or street-based sex work. Rather, the advantages are conferred by and due to the ways in which this society perceives and (marginally) provides protections for certain kinds of sex work.[32]

When we investigate a sex worker's work environment as a measure of safety, it is important for us to understand how the internet has also provided a measure of safety. Not all websites used by sex workers are used for screening clients, however. The widespread availability of webcams and camera phones has allowed some sex workers the chance to work from home, generate content, and access a far greater pool of potential customers without the risk often associated with providing direct services. Websites such as OnlyFans and ManyVids have allowed online performers to create a scalable business for their online content. In some cases, online performers can create an anonymous persona, completely concealing their identity in an effort to avoid the stigma associated with sex work. The privilege of anonymous profiles, however, is also embedded in an oppressive context of classism, racism, and transphobia. Internet access and the ability to afford high-speed internet is a class issue that does not allow some sex workers the ability to engage in internet-based labor. Working at home in the same space as a partner or children (due to the COVID-19 pandemic or an inability to afford a separate space) may not allow for some sex workers to do certain types of work for fear of stigma. These gaps in labor protection are often not talked about in labor rights conversations for sex workers. In addition, such anonymous websites are often afforded only to White or White-passing cisgender performers. They rarely provide the income associated with performers who are willing to show their face. These various hardships make internet-based sex work difficult for some who are motivated by safety and try to engage in it.

When studying who sex workers are, locations and organizations of their work may also determine their risk for certain health concerns. That is, these various locational and organizational aspects of sex work have implications for understanding well-being in terms of encountering and coping with work-environment-related stressors. For example, there are sex workers who are at a higher risk of HIV and STIs because of the discrimination faced in medical centers based on their gender, economic status, and sexual orientation, and because they are sex workers. For example, "47.9% reported harassment and 28.9% were refused treatment by medical providers."[33] Also, researchers studying men who have sex with men (MSM) and who also engaged in sex work reported that their research participants had more medical mistrust and health care discrimination due to issues beyond MSM behavior/identity (e.g., homelessness, substance use, poverty).[34] In short, individuals at lower levels of the whorearchy receive less and less quality care the further down the hierarchy they reside. In turn, the lower levels of care create lower levels of health. These discrepancies create obstacles in receiving basic health care but also cause a mistrust that can deter sex workers from testing and treatments for STIs and HIV.

The presence or absence of organizational management (e.g., club owners, pimps, etc.) to buffer unwanted, work-related harassment is another factor stemming from a sex worker's location of work. The limited studies addressing such environmental and organizational facets have focused on small case studies of high-end workers, such as escorts or call girls serving elite, high-paying clientele.[35] These studies suggest that street-based sex work is a form of survival that often results in lower rates of worker health, whereas sex work historically associated with "higher classes" is a potential profession and career that often results in higher rates of worker health.[36] This limited number of research studies also fails to address the protective factors of sex work's various forms.[37] In short, the location of work for someone working in the sex industry may tell us something about their mental health needs as a sex worker—not because the location predicts identity, but because it can predict safety, access to resources, and support.

Legislation and Oppression

In chapter 1, you were introduced to sex workers not just by defining their work, but by learning about the context and systems in which sex workers are embedded. As we learn more about who sex workers are, it is important for us to learn about how larger systems of oppression can provide us more possible information about who sex workers may be. As you learned in the last chapter, these systems create inaccurate ways of understanding sex workers. One specific example that we want to address more comprehensively is legal systems, which have impacted decisions about legal rights for sex workers, which in turn also eventually impact mental health services. One of the biggest barriers to sex workers' rights and safety is current laws in a variety of countries around the globe that dictate whether sex work is fully legal, is legal in certain contexts and a criminal offense in others, is fully criminalized, or is fully decriminalized. Juno Mac, who started her career as a sex worker in a brothel, is now an advocate in the sex-worker-rights movement to keep sex workers safe. Mac identified five common legal structures designed to regulate sex work in places around the globe:[38]

Full Criminalization. Many countries around the globe, including South Africa, most of the United States, and parts of the Russian Federation, regulate sex work by inflicting criminal charges on all persons involved, including those who purchase sex work, those who sell sex, and involved outside parties. Many lawmakers hope that making sex work illegal will deter people from engaging with it. However, many sex workers choose to break such laws and sell sex because they need to pay bills and feed their family. If convicted, people who have been criminalized are often unable to get other types of work because they now have a criminal record. Consequently, these workers are often forced to pay bribes to and undergo mistreatment by police officers.[39]

Partial Criminalization. Partial criminalization is used in countries including Mexico, Brazil, Egypt, Saudi Arabia, Finland, Spain, France, and the United Kingdom. This legal structure results in buying and selling sex being legal; however, selling sex on the street, brothel keeping, and soliciting sex using online platforms are illegal. Increasingly, advocates for sex workers' rights argue that this legal structure equates to lawmakers stating, "Selling sex is fine—just make sure it is done alone and behind closed doors."[40] In some countries, brothel keeping is defined as having more than one sex worker in a location, complicating the idea of doing sex work "alone." Thus, a sex worker who wants to work in tandem with another sex worker for safety reasons (in one of their homes, for example) could face legal ramifications for the work. Furthermore, the prohibiting of selling sex on the street often results in sex workers being forced to sell sex in hidden locations where they are more susceptible to violence.[41]

The Nordic Model. The Nordic model, used in countries such as Sweden and Canada, attempts to support individuals who sell sex and inflict criminal charges only on those who purchase it. The Nordic model attempts to provide support services to both help sex workers exit the industry and also try to reduce the demand for sex work and inflict fines on the buyers of sexual goods and services.[42] However, people who are selling sex may not have other alternatives for work due to a variety of factors (such as a criminal record, immigration status, need to work certain hours to care for their family, and/or countless other reasons). Thus, reducing the number of buyers by fining them results in sex workers having to offer sex for reduced fees, offer services that place them at greater risk (in order to get paid), or both. In addition, some workers, as a result of not having enough buyers, may increasingly seek the use of a pimp—an individual of any gender who secures buyers for sex workers and arranges the location and other details, in exchange for a portion of the profit. At the time of writing, there is no evidence that this legal structure is effective at decreasing the amounts of sex work in a targeted geographic area, and the level of sex work has not been shown to decrease in countries that adopt it.[43]

Legalization. Sex work is legal in Germany, the Netherlands, and parts of Nevada in the United States, but sex workers must comply with mandated health checks and registration.[44] In addition, sex workers can work only in legally designated areas. Although legal regulation of sex work protects some rights for sex workers, registration can be very expensive, time consuming, and difficult. If an individual is not registered—for example, the person is an undocumented resident and cannot register—the result can be expensive fines or even imprisonment. Through a lens of oppression and marginalization (we reviewed these terms in chapter 1), the most marginalized individuals are often forced to engage in the riskiest and most dangerous kinds of sex work because they cannot comply with regulations (or pay the registration fees) required by the legalization structure.

Within the United States specifically, at the time of this writing, sex work is considered illegal in forty-nine of fifty states. Although criminalizing and punishment of sex work do exist in other states (and differ from state to state), the state of Nevada contains ten counties in which licensed brothels are able to operate under firm guidelines. Nevada is the only state that contains such counties in which some forms of sex work are legal. According to Nevada state law, "It is unlawful for any person to engage in prostitution or solicitation except in a licensed house of prostitution."[45] In addition, the legal structure of legalization requires "forced health checks," such as the mandate that sex workers must use condoms.[46] In addition, legalization forces sex workers to test weekly for sexually transmitted diseases (STDs) and to receive tests monthly for HIV.[47, 48] For these ten counties in Nevada in which sex work is legal, money earned by many of these sex workers often goes back into the communities that serve and protect them.[49] As an example, many sex workers who did work during the COVID-19 pandemic often provided support to members of their community who could not work due to health and safety concerns. In addition, sex workers who did work were able to provide support to individuals who work peripherally in the industry—such as bookkeepers, bartenders, security, etc.—who also felt the impact of closure due to the COVID-19 pandemic.

Decriminalization. In 2003, New Zealand decriminalized sex work at a larger systemic level. The legal structure of decriminalization removes laws and erotophobic registration that punitively target sex workers.[50] Decriminalization of sex work is not the same as making it legal, although many people confuse the two legal structures.[51] Examples of the difference between decriminalization and legalization are that, under decriminalization, individuals who employ sex workers are accountable to the state (instead of having only sex workers be accountable to the state, as in legalization), and a sex worker can refuse to see a client at any time for any reason.[52] If sex work or some elements of it are decriminalized, governments may still choose to define these acts as infractions of civil or administrative law. Decriminalization, however, is an expression of a government's or a society's view that sex work should not be punished by the harshest penalties and that sex workers should not be cast as criminals. In this legal structure, sex workers have rights, and they often belong to collective labor unions and centers of advocacy that support them.

FOSTA-SESTA

Compounded with these legal structures are specific policy acts enacted within the United States that have greatly impacted sex workers. In 2018, the United States Senate and House of Representatives voted two bills into law: the Stop Enabling Sex Traffickers Act (SESTA) and Allow States and Victims to Fight Online Sex Trafficking Act (FOSTA). These bills called for "the Secretary of Health and Human Services to conduct a study to assess the unintended impacts on the health and safety of people engaged in transactional sex, in connection with the enactment of the Allow States and Victims to Fight Online Sex Trafficking Act of 2017 (Public Law 115–164) and the loss of interactive computer services that host information related to sexual exchange, and for other purposes."[53] Although lawmakers originally constructed these as two separate bills, together the bill proclaims that online websites and platforms can be held to be unlawful for user-generated content that is deemed "unlawful."[54] The writers of FOSTA-SESTA clarified that it was then illegal to willingly assist, facilitate, or support sex trafficking. Much of the initiation and support of these laws came from reviews and statistics of child-focused sex trafficking. In addition to the effectiveness of this law's ability to stop sex traffickers coming into question, it has also had a hugely negative impact on many sex workers and their communities, with a disproportionate impact of FOSTA-SESTA on LGBTQ+ sex workers and sex workers of color.[55] Without warning, many websites that provided safe spaces for sex workers to advertise their goods and services swiftly shut down, even though the law was specifically geared toward sex trafficking.

The somewhat vague language of the law resulted in many being not sure if certain advertised services would be considered unlawful, resulting in many sex workers losing numerous clients and safe spaces to promote their businesses. Specifically, the law has resulted in many sex workers losing access to online safety resources and facing financial hardship.[56] Although the law has had a severely negative impact on consensual sex workers, it has not yet seen the abolishment of sex trafficking as it had originally intended.[57] Similar consequences of the law's enactment have been reported internationally.

These various legal stressors result in sex workers combating additional work-related stress for fear of legal fines, worrying about having their safety compromised as internet-based sources close, and fearing police brutality (to name a few). Instead of researching these larger, macro-level influences on sex workers' mental health, many researchers continue to focus on the same tired, archaic questions related to trauma symptoms with no consideration of environment or context. The advent of the internet brought many changes to the field, such as the presence of sites such as *Eros* and *The Erotic Review,* and allowed sex workers great opportunities to advertise their services and screen potential clients. Legislation, however, has presented many issues for sex workers and has threatened to revoke many of the risk-mitigating safety measures afforded to them by these sites. Enacted in 2018, FOSTA-SESTA was presented as a law designed to target online sex trafficking. The law, however, has done far more to damage safety methods designed to protect consensual sex workers from potentially dangerous clients. In 2020, Senator Elizabeth Warren introduced a bill calling FOSTA-SESTA into question for its "unintended impacts on the health and safety of people engaged in transactional sex."[58]

In addition, many sex-for-money-focused websites are also under attack under the proposed Stop Internet Sexual Exploitation Act, also known as SISEA. Proposed in December 2020 by Senators Jeff Merkley (D-Ore.) and Ben Sasse (R-Neb.) and still under review at the time of this writing, SISEA proposed to draw stringent guidelines for all nude and/or explicit content distributed online. Under the laws that would be established by the bill, websites containing content deemed as pornographic would be subject to fines for any content that could be stored as a retrievable data file.[59] Similarly to FOSTA-SESTA, SISEA's name implies that, if passed, it would work to stop online distribution of materials containing images of exploited individuals. However, many online performers were quick to notice that many of the restrictions proposed would target consensual online sex workers and digital pornography and were quick to oppose the bill. Much like the Nordic model and FOSTA-SESTA as described above, SISEA could lead to more of an underground and unsafe environment for sex workers in the future.

These various legal structures and recent mandates help us to see an even more complex picture about who sex workers are. Not only should we position their work within a labor rights movement, but we must position their professional identities within a context of political and legal systems of erotophobia. Unfortunately, when we do not look at a larger context of oppression and discrimination but stay within an outdated, myopic view of morality, we miss many facets that describe the resilience of communities of sex workers within the industry.

A Bigger (Clearer) Picture

So, we have provided you with some definitions in the previous chapter about what sex work is. Further, we wanted to also provide more information about *who sex workers are*. Throughout this chapter, we have helped you see the many factors that influence the description of sex-worker communities, such as cultural identity, workplace environment, and the whorearchy. We have also introduced you to the larger context in which sex workers are embedded that greatly influence the description of who they are, such as legal structures, political mandates, and economic experiences that help to add greater complexity to and a fuller, richer description of those who work in the sex industry. Further, we hope that your understanding of who sex workers are is also rooted in a labor rights movement. This movement helps to highlight parts of the work that mental health providers often do not see and subsequently fail to bring in to their clinical process. In the end, there are an infinite number of issues affecting sex-worker communities, issues that impact sex workers in the United States.

We want to end this chapter identifying two practical strategies for all of us (especially those of us who are mental health workers) to dismantle the whorearchy in various domains of our professional practice. We will be discussing this dismantling in other parts of this book, but for now: one of the best ways to dismantle the whorearchy is to provide examples that discredit it. Showing ways that sex workers do not neatly fit into "classes" or "categories" begins to highlight the flaws in the whorearchy. Further, we can honor and support the resilience and collectivism within groups and communities of sex workers within our practice. Such prioritizing of these protective factors inherently dismantles the whorearchy by combating the oppressions and marginalization that many people use to keep the whorearchy in place. These are just two strategies, and we look forward to sharing more in other parts of this book. However, before we provide more of these practical strategies to use in your clinical work, we need to look backward before we move forward.

3

HISTORICAL PERSPECTIVES OF SEX WORK IN MENTAL HEALTH PRACTICE

*In 2013, I saw a therapist for a very short period of time who was prob-
lematic over this, over my sex work; she was very judgmental, and she
knew there were other things that were happening in my life and with
my family. But she was pointing towards my sex work in that regard, as
the issue. And then, I was working, you know, and my daughter and my
grandson encountered Child Services at one point, and so the social
worker that I was dealing with definitely very much pointed towards my
working in the industry as being problematic in general.*

—SINNAMON

AS WE HAVE NOW reviewed the importance of training about sex work
across the professional lifespan for clinicians, as well as important language
and terminology in sex-work communities, you may be wondering, *"How
did we get here?"* That is, how did various mental health disciplines get to
a place of complete misunderstanding about sex work as well as about the
subsequent harm that occurs in mental health services for sex workers?
As is true with many mental health workers, like the one described by our

consultant Sinnamon in the above excerpt, much of the answer lies in an unchecked history within research and scholarship about the mental health of sex workers. In this chapter, we will ask, *"How have unchallenged historical understandings of sex work created problematic frameworks in which providers engage?"*

In order for us to answer these questions, we will dive deep into the research within various mental health disciplines and related fields. This chapter might read differently than others in this text, in part because there is a lot of research reviewed. Specifically, there are many studies that have contributed to the current state of mental health practice with clients who work in the sex industry. Specifically, we will address not only how flawed methodologies in sex-work research have resulted in oppressive mental health services, but also how a lack of systematic inclusion related to issues of power, privilege, and oppression throughout mental health work has influenced research with sex workers.

Social Science Researchers, Changing Languages, and Flawed Methodologies

When we are beginning to understand the impact of history on current misunderstandings of sex work, it is important for us to first look at language. Although *sex work* is the acceptable term in current literature (as you read about in chapter 2), earlier mental health literature mentions "prostitutes," "streetwalkers," and "hookers."[1, 2] In addition, historical analyses of sex work were limited in the scope of sexuality-focused labor researched, focusing on specific jobs of "street work, ship work, parlor work, escort work, working independently, mistressing, peep show work, stripping, telephone work and topless dancing."[3] Researchers have more recently expanded this definition to encompass other work-related activities, including those discussed in the previous two chapters. Contemporary scholars have infused technological advances into the definition of sex work, noting that moving sex work from the street to the internet has allowed sex work to enter laborers' homes, therefore allowing for the purchase of sex work to be more anonymous. However, such advances are not without additional stigma, which is evident in many of the studies and much of the literature that we consume today.

"So, where did all of this negativity come from?" The short answer is: It in part started with research. In addition to language, current literature outlining how many mental health practitioners understand sex work most often utilizes a theoretical perspective that focuses on understanding human behavior from a model of mental illness, stress, and abnormal/maladaptive behavior.[4] For sex workers, this perspective, called the *oppressive paradigm* by many sex-positive sex-work researchers, suggests that sex work is an "expression of patriarchal gender relations and male domination."[5] The oppressive paradigm often suggests that sex workers are called to sex work because they themselves have mental illness, and that sex work is problematic because individuals who sell sex must have unresolved issues, conflicts, or concerns. Further, using such a perspective creates an understanding of sex work as inherently exploitative and harmful to workers.[6, 7] Ronald Weitzer noted that such an understanding "is responsible for the rise of a resurgent mythology of [sex work]"[8] and creates illness-focused practices that prevent social service providers from fully understanding sex workers' stressors.

When using the oppressive paradigm to study mental health in sex work more in depth, researchers adopting this paradigm may lead mental health professionals to fail to assess and support sex workers' coping skills (instead, just looking for problems). Many of these research studies also portray sex workers as mentally sick, unable to keep other jobs, and abnormal in their routine behavior. This paradigm also creates an adversarial relationship between sex workers and legal bodies, which in turn mandate that sex work should be illegal due to its perceived "problematic" impact within society.[9] When defining the construct of "abnormality" to view behavior, scholars have noted deviance, distress, dysfunction, and danger—all tenets of the oppressive paradigm.[10] Scholars also have written that mental health practitioners in many mental health disciplines such as psychology,[11] social work,[12] marriage and family therapy,[13] and professional counseling[14] often look at marginalized communities such as sex workers from a medical model, focusing on individual and within-community pathology without taking into account these individuals' and communities' strengths and resilience factors.

So, now we can start to see that stigmatization of sex workers in the mental health field in part came from social science. Unfortunately, this need to medicalize and subsequent misunderstandings have had a far-reaching impact on health care providers' learning about sex work. Some more contemporary sex-positive scholars think of the oppressive paradigm as a parasite, eating away at the possibility of true understanding about sex work and perpetuating outdated, inaccurate information that views sex work as a problem. An accurate understanding of the oppressive paradigm helps practitioners to review research of the sex-work industry using a series of conceptual critiques.[15, 16] These critiques highlight problems with studies that focus on sex-worker illness but leave out strengths and resilience factors. Some of these factors include sex workers' ability to seek and receive both formal (i.e., medical and legal assistance) and informal (i.e., emotional support from family and friends) assistance.[17]

In addition to conceptual critiques, deconstructing the oppressive paradigm also results in critiques of methodologies in existing mental health research with sex workers. Weitzer noted that "[d]ata collection procedures in studies based on the oppression paradigm are often either invisible or problematic."[18] Specifically, many studies in mental health fields focused on sex workers often used flawed research methods. For example, studies investigating the human functioning and behavior of sex workers have not used control groups or comparison samples to compare the psychological distress of sex workers with those symptoms found in the overall population.[19] For example, when studying anxiety symptoms in a group of sex workers, researchers should also find a group of non–sex workers (called a control group) with whom they can compare. Indeed, only when a study includes a control group can researchers determine whether a sex worker's job has a significant effect on such anxiety symptoms; having a control group can reduce their possibility of making an erroneous conclusion. This flawed method of design in sex-work studies inherently pathologizes sex workers and provides an inaccurate understanding of sex-worker functioning, career choice, and self-efficacy.

Scholars[20] have also reported other flawed methods. One such method is convenience sampling, or when a researcher collects data from a sample of people that is easy to reach, in many different studies about sex workers' mental health. Such sampling methods illuminate a lack of rigor in sample recruitment and selection processes in mental health research focused on sex workers. For example, many researchers collect data from sex workers who work exclusively on the street, or street-based sex workers (SBSWs), as opposed to samples that include workers in a range of locations (e.g., brothels, sole proprietors via the internet, cam workers, talklines). Many of these SBSWs are in lockdown/incarceration facilities (or they have been in these facilities in the past), adding to their exposure to violence, legal-related stress, and vicarious trauma. In the oppressive paradigm, researchers will analyze data from a sample of SBSWs and make inaccurate generalizations about all sex workers in all locations. If job location (and corresponding safety) may increase resilience for sex workers, it is questionable as to why researchers are not addressing differences in these job duties and locations. Such convenience sampling has also resulted in inaccurate assumptions about the heterogeneity of commercial sex workers, which may cause limitations in applying studies' results to clinical practice.[21]

As if lack of control groups and convenience sampling were not enough, researchers of sex work have also applied the oppressive paradigm to the creation of hierarchies of sex workers. In chapter 2, we presented several hierarchy-based classification systems that researchers have historically used when studying sex work. These hierarchies have permeated the mental health literatures and present a range of value-based labels that demonstrate how sex workers in certain jobs are ascribed more illness and treated with less respect. Sex-positive critiques of these hierarchies raise questions through a lens of cultural privilege. For example, most of the literature using these hierarchies applies only to female sex workers. Many empirical studies written before 1985 do not note how the inclusion of male, transgender, nonbinary, and agender sex workers (or sex workers of additional gender identities and expressions) may impact prevalence rates.[22, 23] Researchers have indicated that discrimination against transgender individuals in traditional job markets leads to a high proportion of them to engage in sex work.[24] As such, hierarchies based on discriminatory "classes" are part of the oppressive paradigm and do not address why there is a disproportionate number of both those individuals assigned female at birth and those who have transitioned their gender and/or sex to female who engage in sex work.[25] Further, these hierarchies begin to make inaccurate assumptions about (and subsequently fail to explain) why women of color are disproportionately represented in sex work,[26] demonstrating how sociocultural factors such as race intersect with gender and gender identity to skew understandings of prevalence rates using culturally biased research frameworks and research designs. These various conceptual and methodological flaws illustrate how the oppressive paradigm can inaccurately lead clinicians to focus on the wrong topics in their clinical work.

Feminists' Historical Critiques of Sex Work

As you are reading, you are probably beginning to see how flawed methods have created flawed research, which in turn has created flawed understandings of sex work. In addition to flawed research, the oppressive paradigm has resulted in many heated debates about sex work that have also resulted in clinicians' increased biases. In one core example, feminist mental health practitioners and activists have historically and heatedly debated stances toward sex work and the sex industry.[27, 28, 29, 30] Writers have historically described this division between stances as "a split between an emphasis on sexual freedom and pleasure that views women exclusively as agents . . . and an emphasis on sexual danger and degradation that sees women exclusively as victims."[31] These debates continue to some degree in current feminist scholarship and practice, resulting in many divisions within mental health practitioners.

These scholars have categorized the feminist perspective regarding sex work as falling into two distinct stances. Historically, many feminists believed in an older perspective that all forms of sex work were a type of patriarchal control over and an exploitation of women. This first stance of feminist approaches is against sex work, viewing it as "coercion and sexual subordination." The second stance, containing liberal feminist and sex-positive approaches, takes an affirming approach to sex work, arguing that sex work is a job, much like any other, and can be a form of self-determination for all women-identified people.[32] This newer stance creates a framework of sex work as an inevitable market exchange and an expression of women's own sexual agency. Many advocates for sex work agree that such discord between the two feminist approaches is useful in that it resists making judgments about sex workers themselves while still challenging the perceptions of the industry in general.[33] The many biased research studies discussed earlier in this chapter often fuel this debate.

When we consider *"How did we get here?"* it is vital for us to think about how research-induced hierarchies helped to create the gender discrepancy within the sex-work industry. This discrepancy lays the groundwork for a language that ignores gender diversity within sex work that devalues women, ignores these workers' self-determination, and views entry into the profession as forced. For example, an issue that feminists have highlighted in the past is the use of the word *girls* (e.g., call girls, in-house girls) in the labeling of sex workers. Historical references to women-identified sex workers as girls[34] have exacerbated the exploitation of these workers and their clients. In another example, much of the literature focused on the feminist debates related to sex work introduced a discrepancy of focusing only on female-identified people in the field. The small body of literature focusing on male sex workers[35] has historically suggested that there are often conflicting ideas about why male-identified people entered into sex work, including a poorly experienced and underdeveloped sense of personal and economic power.

Understanding historical, gendered notions of sex work can help mental health practitioners to understand shame and stigma for non-female-identified sex workers that may lead to a rejection of their own strengths and empowerment. These topics are often left out of the research that clinicians consume. Instead of addressing shame and stigma related to cultural and societal oppression of sex work (whorephobia), the research leads us to believe that the "illness" and distress are caused by sex workers' participation in the industry (which is not true). These analyses help to illuminate the bias and oppression caused by research and scholarship in the oppressive paradigm. These biases within the literature result in researchers making inaccurate assumptions about different parts of the sex industry. One major inaccurate assumption is the reasons for entering sex work.

Reasons for Entering Sex Work: Examples of the Oppressive Paradigm

In the beginning of this chapter, we asked you, *"How have unchallenged historical understandings of sex work created problematic frameworks in which providers engage?"* When going back to this question, you may already begin to see the answer: Research with a lot of bias created a baseline of illness and stigma. Unfortunately, other research addressing specific issues related to sex work built upon this research to create—you guessed it—more faulty research. One specific issue where we see such building upon the oppressive paradigm is research that focuses on sex workers' entry into the industry.

Although researchers have investigated individuals' entry into the sex-work industry, many researchers have assumed such entry as illness-driven. Harry Benjamin and Robert Masters[36] wrote an early, sickness-based conceptualization that addressed individuals' reasoning to enter the sex-work industry. They categorized female sex workers into two broad groups: (1) *Voluntary:* women who have voluntarily entered into "the life" by free choice, and (2) *Compulsive:* women who are compelled to do so by their own psychoneurotic needs, which is a false and useless dichotomy. Much later, writers and scholars identified predisposing factors that they believed led cisgender women into sex work, including separation from caretakers, parental promiscuity, childhood trauma, domestic violence, substance abuse, and loss of life.[37] Within mental health disciplines, scholars historically have published studies suggesting other reasons that sex workers enter the field. Such reasons include ability to fund existing drug use,[38] access to basic needs such as shelter,[39] introduction by a friend or family member involved in sex work to the sex-work industry,[40, 41] and lack of knowledge surrounding other career and/or vocational options that may better suit their interests.[42]

As you probably guessed, several biased assumptions and methodological flaws inhabit these previous writings on entry into sex work. Many of the researchers conducting these studies use convenience sampling (mentioned earlier in this chapter) that often results in a lack of representation across the sex-worker hierarchy and various locations of sex work. In writings on the oppressive paradigm, Weitzer noted that young age of entry into prostitution is a myth that scholars have disputed for many years, dating back to early scholars.[43] Other scholars[44] have also refuted current notions of entry into the sex-work field, noting that the entrance into these various types of labor can be spurred by a combination of social and economic factors and not because of familial discord or an individual's possible traumatic history (as some writings have suggested). These authors instead suggest that current economic needs, opportunities, and other situational adult factors better explain workers' involvement in the sex industry.[45]

Such skewed conceptualizations often result in mental health practitioners' inaccurate assumptions about why sex workers enter the field. Mental health practitioners then see the sex worker as a female who entered the field because of some past sickness. These clinical applications also render male and transgender sex workers as invisible, unable to be studied, or unable to have competent services provided for them.[46] Such biases allow mental health practitioners to reject the notions that men can enter sex work, be in positions of subordination, or hire other men for sexual services.

Reasons for Entering Sex Work: Resilience/Empowerment Paradigm

So, you may be asking, *"What should we do instead?"* That is, when clinicians are trying to understand how a client's entry into sex work may be a part of their treatment, how might clinicians shift their lens? A clear first answer is that research about sex workers' mental health needs to shift its lens. Instead of a psychopathology-based paradigm of sex work, a resilience- and empowerment-focused lens might help researchers to focus on the economics by which individuals attempt to gain employment and support themselves. For example, increasing numbers of university students are entering sex work in response to the increasing costs of tuition and fees, and the reduction of government financial support.[47, 48] Traditional means of employment typically consist of long hours and low wages, often failing to adequately compensate for tuition alone, not to mention living expenses. For this reason, some students are now resorting to legal or illegal jobs that require fewer hours and offer considerably higher wages, allowing them more time for classes and studying as well as the ability to support themselves financially. For many people, these factors make entering the sex-work industry a viable option.[49]

In addition to economics, another way to shift the research lens about entry into sex work is a focus on social support. More recent literature has suggested that individuals enter the sex-work industry for social support of various kinds. Mental health practitioners have noted the importance of social support as an aspect of resilience,[50] and such resilience could be helpful for sex workers navigating dangerous and stress-inducing work environments. Many sex workers may lack social support on a variety of ecological and systemic levels[51] and may enter more collective work environments (e.g., a brothel versus working independently) to gain such social support. In the past, scholars have reported that a lack of social support correlated with discrimination against sex workers based on sex,[52] gender,[53] race,[54] ethnicity,[55] and socio-economic status.[56] Aside from showing how this lack of social support may correlate with cultural identity, much of the mental health literature has not addressed social support as a specific area of study, which has undoubtedly impacted how clinicians integrate social support into their assessment and treatment planning with their clients who work in the sex industry.

In addition, the need to access social support from other sex workers raises the question as to why sex workers are not accessing additional outside resources as a form of coping. Scholars[57] have noted that sex workers rarely access social support outside of other sex workers, and therefore may be initially attracted to certain types of collective work environments for the safety and community that they provide. Researchers have noted that these types of work environments are particularly attractive to a sex worker if the individual experiences isolation or discrimination in other areas of life.[58] More specifically, such social support has been found to help buffer the discriminatory services that sex workers have experienced from social service providers, including legal services, police, social services, and mental health services.[59] These studies suggest that street-based sex work is a form of survival, whereas high-end sex work is a potential profession and career, and that support is an important factor.[60, 61] We will talk more about different examples of such support in future chapters of this book.

Your review of these historical literatures may result in more questions than answers. Specifically, mental health researchers still know little concerning overarching trends of why individuals tend to enter sex work. Further, a review of research suggests that there are many perceived reasons for individuals to enter sex work; however, researchers utilizing the oppressive paradigm inaccurately suggest that people enter sex work because of their past trauma or pathology. Future research on social support in sex-work communities should combat these false narratives by investigating how resilience factors (e.g., availability of social support, ability to ask for help, etc.) impact entry into sex work (versus pathologizing an individual for entering the industry).

Such research would in turn impact clinicians' focus on social support networks in their clinical work. Clinicians reading the forementioned studies and articles are often left with the idea that their primary treatment goal should be to "assist" their client in leaving the industry (more on this in later chapters of this book). In addition, these inaccurate studies also lead clinicians to focus on psychopathology and mental health symptoms in sex workers *that the clinician begins to believe have been caused by (or led to) their desire to enter sex work.*

So, you are now realizing that faulty baseline assumptions in mental health research have led to even more faulty research—in this case, specifically about the reasons that people enter sex work. However, the problem is less like a telephone pole and much more like a large tree. The oppressive paradigm is the root, and there are numerous branches of this tree that have grown. If entry into sex work is one large branch, various mental health diagnoses of sex workers are another branch. Researchers have thoroughly examined these diagnoses in mental health literature from multiple disciplines. And the oppressive paradigm Weitzer used in mental health research about diagnosis of sex workers results in generalizing worst cases to the entire sex-worker population.[62] However, a discussion of resilience factors in the analysis of these diagnoses is noticeably absent. To say that individuals who are in the sex-work industry have no mental health diagnoses would be inaccurate. However, the oppressive paradigm inaccurately portrays prevalence rates of these diagnoses without comparing sex workers to the general population. To provide a more comprehensive example, we will review two of the largest diagnoses found in sex-work literatures: drug and alcohol abuse and trauma.

Sex Work, the Oppressive Paradigm, and Drug and Alcohol Use

One of the most widely discussed diagnoses in sex-work research in mental health disciplines is alcohol and drug abuse. Much of the literature historically[63, 64, 65] has shown high positive associations between involvement in sex work and use of alcohol and other drugs. Illness-focused frameworks have held the view that drug use was a gateway into the sex-work industry (interestingly, these studies referenced only women-identified sex workers).[66, 67] In the past, many of these authors have noted that sex workers living with addiction work in the sex trade to get money to support their own usage when few other sources of income are available to them. Studies that investigated drug use among sex workers have found that sex workers were found to have a significantly higher severity of drug use and were more likely to use drugs to (1) increase confidence, control, and closeness to others; and (2) decrease feelings of guilt.[68, 69]

When concurrently reviewing these studies and deconstructing the oppressive paradigm, one sees methodological flaws in these findings, including that some of these and similar studies generalize worst-case scenarios to the entire sex-worker population. As you read about earlier in this chapter, many of these researchers also conduct studies using sex workers who work in certain jobs and in certain locations and make inaccurate generalizations about all sex workers based on these specific groups. Further, the lack of control groups in some studies often calls into question the results of those studies. Although there is a common myth that sex workers may enter the field in order to fund their drug use, a small group of studies with more rigorous methodologies suggests that sex workers likely start or increase their drug use in order to deal with distress caused by activities associated with their occupation. In fact, research that is more recent has suggested that many sex workers used drugs or alcohol as a way to cope with the trauma and work-related stress that they experienced since entering into the field.[70, 71]

Additionally, there is a dearth of literature focusing on sex workers' use of drugs or alcohol to cope with their work-related stress. For example, one study that is more contemporary has indicated that female sex workers may feel stigma and shame from the way that their children view their work, as many prostitutes are mothers, and therefore use substances to cope.[72] Unfortunately, this study alone may not be a match for the overarching, oppressive narrative about sex workers' drug use. In reality, this narrative is often overlooked but important, as persons engaged in sex work are often blamed for social problems or perceived as victims.[73] Such negative connotations often result in sex workers avoiding the disclosure of what they do for work and referring to sex work as "working" without mentioning sexual aspects of their job.[74] Further, sex workers will often keep their work identity separate from their nonwork identity, which results in worry that someone they know will find out about this work that they do, contributing to the need for substance use to cope. As stated earlier, however, an articulation of sex workers' positive coping mechanisms to deal with these issues is almost entirely absent from the mental health literature.

These analyses highlight how research on substance use and abuse for sex workers is often inherently flawed. Thus, the literature used by clinicians to inform their practice neglects the resilient efforts of sex workers to cope with work-related stress and harsh work environments, and to get and/or remain sober. The literature that does reflect such resilience and strength-based understandings of sex work often misinterprets or misrepresents the reality of sex workers in ways similar to what has been described above. Also significant is the dearth of literature on the topic of sex workers' recovery from substance abuse. Further, reporting more comprehensively on relationships between sex work and drug/alcohol abuse is crucial to help sex workers more fully who wish to do addiction and recovery work as part of their mental health treatment.

Trauma and Post-Traumatic Stress: Constructing Paradigm Shifts

When reviewing historical literature that identifies psychopathology in sex workers, trauma is another one of the largest diagnoses studied. Scholars have documented a variety of different trauma symptoms of sex workers, including post-traumatic stress disorder (PTSD).[75, 76, 77] Studies investigating mental health symptoms of female sex workers have documented that, on average, approximately two-thirds of their respective samples of sex workers met the full criteria for symptoms of PTSD. Scholars have historically tried to deconstruct these symptoms, speculating that sex workers often experience a form of "psychological paralysis" that prevents them from taking an active role in their lives.[78] Participants in one study[79] reported that many of these symptoms were exacerbated or reinforced by conditions in their current work environments, including rape (reported by 62 percent), assault (73 percent), and being threatened with a weapon (68 percent). In a noteworthy study on trauma and PTSD in sex-work communities, the

Prostitution and Research Education Project of San Francisco Women's Centers[80] surveyed 475 sex workers in the United States, South Africa, Thailand, Turkey, and Zambia and found that about two-thirds of sex workers met the full criteria for PTSD; these rates were similar across cultural and national borders among the women surveyed. These studies support the prevalence of PTSD symptoms in sex workers, but *often make inaccurate assumptions about the origin of these symptoms,* neglecting to take dangerous work environments into account.

Other research in mental health disciplines has questioned the origin of these symptoms, but has failed to question the oppressive paradigm from which the illness narrative originated. For example, scholars have examined how the location of one's work impacts trauma-related symptom presentations for sex workers. In a study of female-identified sex workers in Baltimore, Maryland, researchers found that a significant number of the workers met the criteria for PTSD.[81] When investigating such PTSD symptoms, researchers have identified anti-sex-work stigma and financial stress as two of the largest predictors—not necessarily symptoms that started before the worker entered the industry, but symptoms that started due to how the worker was treated once they entered the industry.[82]

Many of the studies that investigate trauma-related symptoms often neglect to state that sex workers have a disproportionate exposure to violence and discrimination at work when compared to people in other service industries. Police violence is a noteworthy and specific component of this exposure to violence. Historically, studies suggest that, of sex-worker participants who survived rape, a range of 17–24 percent were able to name a police officer as a perpetrator of the violence.[83] Scholars have also noted that location of sex work may impact trauma-related symptoms, finding that there was significantly more physical violence for sex workers who seek employment on the streets (as opposed to brothel work, video work, or escort work).[84] The Sex Workers Education and Advocacy Taskforce noted that the sex workers in their study experienced high levels of violence and noted that the criminalized context in which they worked made them exceptionally vulnerable to violence and violence-related trauma.[85] However, the investigation of how sex workers transcend and/or cope with these symptoms is almost absent from the various disciplines of mental health literature.

By now, we are sure that the theme is pretty clear—and it carries over into the research about trauma-related symptoms of sex workers in mental health literature. In short: these psychopathology-focused writings over time provide even more evidence of the oppressive paradigm. Specifically, scholars select the most disturbing examples of trauma symptoms and present them as representative of the entire population of sex workers. With this skewed portrayal is an absence of these workers' exposure to institutionalized violence (e.g., police brutality) and violence from their clients. Further, scholars go on to proclaim inaccurately that these symptoms are indicative of long-standing, intrinsic problems (such as mental illness or PTSD),[86] and that these "lifelong pathologies" are the reason for entry into sex work. Weitzer highlighted that scholars often cast the worst-case scenarios in the sex trade as the norm and ignore those sex workers who do not suffer with acute mental health symptoms.[87] Through a sex-positive lens, those sex workers who present free of pathology are a critical resource for uncovering possible protective factors of ongoing psychological well-being in the sex industry. Further, the need for and documentation of research and practice that highlight such resilience strategies are nascent to absent from the mental health literature.[88]

By studying sex-worker resilience, mental health practitioners may be able to better serve both sex-worker communities as well as other marginalized populations. For example, in an analysis of sex workers in comparison with matched control groups, researchers have suggested that, on average, their sample of street-based sex workers were obliged to "fend for themselves" at an earlier age than non–sex workers in terms of self-care, self-monitoring, and overall developmental support.[89] Mental health researchers should study such "fending for oneself" in order to understand how such resilience factors continue to promote psychological well-being.

A more strength-based, sex-positive analysis of the sex-work literature suggests that rates of PTSD may not stem from an intrinsic lack of mental well-being. Rather, sex workers' experiences of trauma-related symptoms may result from coping with dangerous clients, erotophobia and whorephobia, and oppressive laws and political structures. Further, a resilience-focused lens highlights the need to investigate the association between social support and sex work in increasing the ability to cope with work-induced stressors that cause such trauma. Therefore, researchers need to describe the meaning of community and the support from the community of individuals within the sex-work industry (both within classes of the hierarchy and between classes of the hierarchy).

Putting It Together

At the beginning of this chapter, we asked, *"How did we get here?"* In order to answer this question, we helped to explain the oppressive paradigm as a base from which many systems and theories that impact mental health practice have grown. Analyses and critiques of mental health literature suggest that the current literature that informs clinical practice with sex workers is problematic and builds upon itself. Problems in the research literature focused on sex work include the lack of control groups, convenience sampling that often results in a lack of representation across various jobs and locations of sex work, unmentioned sampling limitations, and poorly developed constructs of investigation. Scholars have noted the importance of involving the participants in the research process through designs such as participatory action research (PAR), which can empower sex workers to demystify their professional field and help to build self-esteem by working to further mental health practitioners' understanding of the phenomena related to sex work.[90, 91] These types of research studies would allow clinicians who consume such research to more accurately hear the mental health needs of sex workers from workers themselves. Many of these studies also have pointed historically to the need for additional theory development regarding intersections between associations and possible mediating relationships of sex work, drug use, trauma, and vocational psychology and career counseling that takes into account the language and hierarchy of sex workers, to provide guidance for designing and analyzing research.

Further, researchers should explore the conditions that affect sex work through a holistic lens rather than focusing on an illness-driven entry into sex work. Such a framework could add to the small number of research studies that address the individual and community protective factors of sex work's various forms. For example, the exploration of the wide range of interpersonal skills and street smarts that facilitate sex workers' survival in an environment that may be violent and strenuous is an area of needed research. Researchers focusing on agency, well-being, and resilience of sex workers need to collect data from samples that include sex workers working in a variety of jobs and occupations rather than focusing solely on the participants who are most convenient or accessible. Such methodological shifts could help researchers to understand how location can help to nurture strengths of sex workers and protect them from job-related stress and hazards. Research addressing how sex workers face mental health risks over the life course could be vital in improving clinical practice with this specific population of clients. Without a methodologically rigorous body of research from which to draw theory, mental health practitioners are not able to make accurate inferences, develop hypotheses, and arrive at implications about and for a group of clients who need services that are more competent.

4

SELF-EXAMINATION OF ATTITUDES TOWARD SEX WORK

....

Padma is a thirty-one-year-old, South Asian, cisgender, heterosexual female licensed marriage and family therapist who has been working in a community mental health agency in Tulsa, Oklahoma, for the last six years. The first two of these six years were before Padma was licensed, and she had been excited to stay at the agency once she became licensed because she wanted to supervise other pre-licensed clinicians. The agency, a nonprofit community mental health agency in East Tulsa, serves many individuals who are in need of mental health services due to sliding-scale, income-based service rates. Padma's newest client is Miriam, also a South Asian, cisgender, heterosexual female, who is coming to therapy to work on her issues of anxiety. During their third session together, Padma asks a series of questions about employment history, as she realizes that Miriam had told her in their initial session that she worked full time, but Padma had not inquired further about Miriam's work. When Padma asks her about her job, Miriam looks at the floor. "I earn a decent living, and I don't think that my job has anything to do with why I feel anxious." Padma continues to ask gently and in different ways until

Miriam looks up from the floor. "I own my own website on OnlyFans," Miriam whispers. "My husband thinks I work remotely for a tech company." Padma nods slowly, and she can feel her face getting slightly warm. Padma begins to wonder why Miriam has not told her husband. She also notices a thought running through her head: "My client is a liar if she lies to her husband...."

IN THE PREVIOUS THREE chapters, we've shared about the interweaving elements that shape the context of how mental health workers understand sex work (and how they bring this faulty understanding into their clinical work). The language, the research, and the history of sex work within multiple countries have resulted in sex workers becoming problematized by many clinicians in various disciplines. Now that we have given you some information about *"How did we get here?"* we want to start to provide a foundation for two additional questions: *"What do we do about it?"* and *"How can we do it differently?"* Specifically, we will begin to shift from theoretical and macro approaches of understanding sex work to a more micro, clinical, and application-focused lens of how these understandings can be a part of clinical practice.

As you have read several times in this book in the previous chapters, a crucial part of how we change clinical practice with clients who are sex workers is to change ourselves as clinicians. It's incumbent on therapists to make these changes, and it is also a difficult topic to incorporate into conversations about clinical work and mental health services. Outside of clinical work, there is a growing movement for all health providers to minimize the potential negative impact of implicit biases on patient care by honoring diversity in the medical profession. With this movement, physician-leaders have clearly identified their responsibility to denounce their biases, to consciously override them, which was not true of their profession historically. In addition, a variety of historical analyses within mental health work have noted that many clinicians from various disciplines or theoretical modalities were also not encouraged or challenged to examine their own biases and to make changes. Indeed, for a long time, clinicians constructed therapeutic contexts in the nineteenth and twentieth centuries in which the clinician was all-knowing, infallible, and not to be questioned.[1] However, in order to make therapeutic spaces in which our clients feel safe to heal and grow, we have to be the ones to change first—including acknowledging and working with our own biases. In this chapter, we focus on the first step in creating sex-positive spaces for clients in the sex industry: acknowledging the bias and judgment that lie within ourselves.

Why Clinicians' Self-Examination Is Important

"Yes, yes. I know, I keep hearing, 'You need to know your own biases.' I get it." Both of us as authors of this book have heard multiple colleagues, supervisees, and leaders in our professional organizations utter these words. We joke with each other that we can often tell when someone "gets it" and yet has not actually done the work of which they claim to "get" the importance. That is, we want to urge you to realize that it's more than "getting it." Some of us may say that we understand the importance of reflecting upon our biases about the sex-work industry and people in it, but we do not actually do the work to know what we think (and what we feel) about a lot of the issues that many of us are socialized not to talk about. Similar to the dynamic of "spiritual bypassing," clinicians can and often do engage in what we informally call "clinical development bypassing." It's our shorthand phrase to describe the ways in which mental health clinicians, willfully or not, act as though there is no need to see personal and professional development as an ongoing practice. Instead, for many different reasons, clinicians may continue to hide behind jargon or "staying true" to their favorite theoretical orientation/modality. However, what we know is that although health care is an inherently data-driven field, most clinicians operate with limited evidence guiding their decisions.[2] Sexuality and sex work are two such topics where many clinicians are not asked to examine their biases (let alone shift them[3]).

Although we may know the importance of acknowledging our biases, we may not know that to do so is not just optimal work and "good practice"— to do so is actually an ethical mandate. Different codes of ethics, such as those from National Association of Social Workers (Standard 4.05[4]), the American Association for Marriage and Family Therapy (Standard 3.3[5]), the American Counseling Association (Standards A.4.a. and A.4.b.[6]), the American Psychological Association (Standard 2.06[7]), and the American

Association of Sexuality Educators, Counselors and Therapists (Principle Two[8]), all state the importance of clinician self-examination as *integral* to the work. As we have listed here, there are lots of codes of ethics, standards, and professional guidelines to indicate that it's not enough to know that we need to self-examine our biases, but that to actively not do so (both talk the talk *and* walk the walk) will harm people. For example, in the vignette above, Padma's nonverbal communication (thinking about Miriam being a liar, and having her body temperature rise) and verbal communication (persistent questioning of Miriam) exemplify the danger of initial denial about biases that may be harmful to the client in a variety of different ways. Although Padma's initial lack of questioning about Miriam's work (until the third session) is an omission that any clinician could make, it is also important to recognize how such an omission may have also "set the stage" for Padma to make assumptions about Miriam's work history, connecting possible biases about sex work with Miriam's racial and gender identities.

In addition, there are copious accounts of clients' experiences in therapy both in the popular press[9, 10] and in empirical literature[11, 12] that highlight the harmful impact of therapists who do not specifically acknowledge their own biases (and how these biases then bleed into other aspects of the clinical process). When focusing on sexuality, the specific voices and perspectives inside and outside of mental health literature of sex workers who have been harmed by therapists who had specific biases against the sex-work industry[13, 14, 15, 16] are unfortunately too many to count. When combined, these various ethical codes and personal accounts send a powerful message: In order to provide mental health services to clients in the sex industry, it's not just about knowing that we need to be different . . . we have to do the work to *be* different.

First Things First: You Are Not Alone

After her third session with Miriam, Padma realizes that she may have some biases about sex work that she might need to examine. As she reflects on colleagues with whom she can talk, she realizes that it may be difficult to talk with someone inside of her agency. Padma recalls several moments with her colleagues during several staff meetings in which her agency's director (who was also Padma's former clinical supervisor) said some derogatory remarks about several clients who were in the sex industry, specifically about the way clients presented themselves (the way that these clients dressed and talked). Upon initial reflection, Padma thinks about confiding in a colleague, Sue Ellen, who works in her agency and got licensed around the same time as Padma. Padma has always considered Sue Ellen, a multiracial (White and Latinx), queer-identified, cisgender woman, relatively open and nonjudgmental about sex. However, as Padma thinks about talking with Sue Ellen, she is instantly filled with self-doubt and shame. What if Sue Ellen judges her for not being more sex positive? What if Sue Ellen feels differently about her for having certain doubts about sex work? Padma decides not to talk with Sue Ellen, as she is worried what the result will be if she confides with Sue Ellen about these areas.

As she reflects further, Padma realizes that there is not anyone within the agency with whom she can talk. As several days go by, Padma realizes that she definitely needs to ensure that she finds someone outside of her immediate agency with whom she can unpack some of her unexamined biases in a space that feels supportive yet can simultaneously hold her accountable for some of the work that she needs to do. As Padma wonders what to do, she begins to feel anxiety in the days leading up to her next session with Miriam, thinking constantly about how she might do harm to the client. Padma begins to wonder if there are other ways that her bias might show, such as her intake report or her case notes for this particular client. As she reviews her notes, Padma realizes that she left the part about Miriam's work in the sex industry out of the case notes for their third session. Upon initial reflection, Padma evaluates her decision as a good decision in order to protect Miriam's privacy. However, as she continues to reflect on the decision, Padma wonders if she left this information out of the case notes due to her own embarrassment or inability to converse about the topic of sex work. She realizes that the same behavior (not including Miriam's job as a sex worker in her clinical notes) could be due to a desire to protect her client's privacy and welfare or it could be because of Padma's own discomfort with sex work, and she realizes how important it is to understand the motive for her decision.

....

The first crucial step to acknowledging bias, erotophobia, and whorephobia is to identify *where we learned such discriminatory and oppressive ideas and practices* (remember these terms from chapters 1 and 2? If not, now might be a good time to return to those chapters and review these terms). As we have learned so far, to state that we are the only ones who have internalized such negative frameworks would be false—in fact, almost all of us live in spaces and contexts that support our learning disgust, shame, and fear about sexuality. That disgust and discomfort are infused into what we, as clinicians, are taught about examining our own attitudes about sexuality in general.

Examples of instances that shape our attitudes about sexuality and sex work include sex education in high school and college, media of various forms as we mention in other chapters such as online and social media, and our graduate training programs to become clinicians. If we take a moment to cast our minds back and look more closely at such training programs, each of us can remember key incidents in our academic classes and/or in our fieldwork placements (practica and internships) that helped us to learn how to think negatively about sex in our clinical work. It may have been a professor or clinical supervisor who said something cringeworthy or pitying and it stuck with us. It may have been a classmate or someone in our supervision group who said something mocking and outlandish against sex workers that no one bothered to question or bring to the attention of the group as problematic. We learned it everywhere. And no one taught us any differently. Knowing some of your own historical context will help to normalize some of your own biases. Remember, there is a difference between normalizing and validating. Just like an eye, a brain, and an anus, we all have one or more biases.

> Sometimes I like to think about how uninformed I was [as an early clinician], and like, Oh, my God, like, who was I seeing at that time? you know? and just to kind of think about what kind of damage I have done. That's painful, right? That's absolutely incredibly painful. And if you could think about what damage have I done in my ignorance? What damage have I done with my overconfidence, my overcommitting? Then I think we find our balance with, how do we need to approach, especially clients that we are not accustomed to working

with? I tell sex workers this all the time: "I take pause with how sex workers are treated in mental health. And so I am sharing that with you because there may have been some things that you will choose to share with me or won't choose to share with me based on previous experiences in mental health that have not been favorable. I'm here to apologize for that and I am here to figure out how we can correct any of the things that have happened. And I'm also here to make sure that we can prevent some of that." It's important to share that I understand that my industry has likely done more harm than good prior to this point.

—JASMINE

What has also occurred is that, no matter what happened in our past, the present context hasn't done anything to correct such biases and assumptions. As one of our consultants, Jasmine, notes above, we often think about the biases that previous versions of ourselves may have had. Perhaps colleagues at our current place of employment have continued to pump erotophobia into the atmosphere of our clinical practice. Perhaps we belong to professional organizations that send out erotophobic messages or brochures about conferences that either contain information about discriminatory practices with sex workers, or that have no programming about sex positivity at all (making silence about sexuality and sex work even more the norm). We strongly encourage you to find some time in your schedule to complete Resource 4.1 (at the end of this chapter) before you continue to read further. This activity will provide you some information to guide you to reflect more comprehensively about your own attitudes and biases and also to do some in-depth exploration of where these biases originated. Normalizing these biases does not make them any less harmful, but it does decrease the isolation and shame that we might feel about these biases.

What we conclude from these difficult histories about sex work is that we have to be okay with acknowledging that all of us have some work to do. We can be expert and/or gifted clinicians and still have a lot of "our own stuff" that we need to bring to the surface, look at, and begin to change. Clinicians' acknowledging and reducing their internal biases is not a linear, short process; rather, it is an ongoing process, an upward spiral, that might last their entire career, engaged with through continuous reflection and action. In our experiences as sexuality educators of clinicians and supervisors, we are often asked, *"How do you know when you have a bias?"* Our answer is simple: It's not always clear the ways in which a bias manifests itself, and it's important to assume that we all have biases. In a similar way, if there is a leak in the pipes of your living space, you may not know, because those leaks are often internal and behind walls. It's the clues that you may get by looking closely at the floors, ceiling, walls, carpeting, furniture, and faucets that help you to realize that something is wrong. It's about intentionally noticing. We suggest that the way to "know" that you have a bias is to get familiar with your thoughts, feelings, and behaviors. As you begin to investigate these parts of yourself, your knowledge about where your bias lies begins to emerge. This knowledge may have common ingredients for all of us, but the unique combination and order of these ingredients might be different for each individual clinician. Further, biased behaviors, thoughts, assumptions, and attitudes may circle our clinical work with different intensities at different times.

One common ingredient that many clinicians speak about is our feelings when we recognize a bias.[17] Such feelings include defensiveness, shame, and guilt. It's almost as though we as therapists think that we are not human, that we do not live in the same world as our clients and family members who are sautéed in the same biases, erotophobia, and whorephobia that we are. As though we don't watch the same TV shows, read the same magazines, click on the same pop-up ads for internet sites, and peruse the same social media posts. But we do. We work in systems that support a culture of shame and isolation when we have biases, in which we can't talk about our biases, instead of finding ways to leverage our relationships to process our biases. Like Padma in the vignette, we feel isolated—either because we do not want to own our biases with our colleagues, or we know that our colleagues might share some of these same biases, which could result in a tarnishing, straining, or destruction of our professional relationships (for example, a colleague retaliating against us because we have indirectly asked that colleague to look at their own respective bias, which could be difficult to do).

So we have to acknowledge that we have such biases, and then actively dismantle them or do something about them. However, what we too often do instead is highly problematic: We ignore the biases, do not acknowledge them, and either overtly or covertly ask clients to hold our shame. Sometimes, our embarrassment about our own bias is so difficult that we implicitly ask our clients to make us feel better. If a client in the sex industry is brave enough to identify a bias that we have (maybe not calling it a bias, but calling attention to something that we have said or done as not feeling good, being inappropriate, being uninformed, etc.), we often make it about our shame in the counseling room and not about the harm that we have done to our clients. We offer apologies that are actually justifications for our own actions disguised with an "I'm sorry about what I said, but ..." tacked to the beginning of our sentence. Clinicians may inadvertently try to justify our biases, which can leave clients feeling confused, angry, resigned, or questioning what is happening in the room. Some clients may also try to make us feel better, especially if they feel indebted to their clinician for work done before the incident in which a bias was revealed. And, because we are ashamed of our bias, we let them. We don't stop them and state, *"I appreciate the sentiment, but you do not have to take care of me in this moment. I made a mistake, and I need to do some work."* We let our clients make us feel better, even though they came to us to feel better in the first place.

In addition, these feelings of shame, guilt, and the resulting lack of accountability consequently lead to our not reaching out for necessary support or education about our own biases and reactions. Further, as these biases become unchecked, we begin to justify them and let them fester. They take root in the soil of our work and begin to infect many different aspects of our work, like weeds or parasites. Quinn Capers IV noted that people in the health professions are not immune to these implicit associations or biases, and that these biases can lead us to unknowingly associate certain demographic groups with negative concepts.[18] Such concepts can emerge rapidly in our work with clients in the sex industry, taking forms like our thinking about sex workers in therapy solely from frames of danger, noncompliance, and lower comprehension and understanding of what is happening in the therapeutic process.[19] These biases can influence clinical decisions (such as diagnosis, case conceptualization, treatment plans, case management, etc.) or result in ways that potentially harm sex workers.[20]

In our work with clients in the sex industry, we have found that our biases do not operate in silos—in fact, we have noticed that these biases often travel in pairs or packs. For example, if Theo has a bias that he learned about sex workers from his educational experiences as an adolescent, he may have other biases about sex workers that he had built on top of the initial biases, like layers of a cake. Having a clinician whom you trust may help you cut all the way through the different layers of a bias . . . cutting into not just your present-day thoughts, but the thoughts and feelings underneath those that may have stemmed from formative, developmental experiences that included depictions of people in the sex industry. In another example, perhaps Jamila has a good friend who is a sex worker, and she starts to create a bias that sex workers have experiences very similar to those of her friend . . . even when they do not. By reducing different experiences into one composite sex-work experience, she may not be able to see the diversity in sex-work experiences (as we spoke about at length in chapters 2 and 3), which may impact how she foresees the remainder of her mental health work with a client. As we see in the work of Padma in the vignette above, bias begins to spread into multiple arenas of clinical work. Specifically, Padma's assumption about Miriam's veracity and Padma's uncertainty about where to find support. Therefore, naming these biases is of the utmost importance as we think about dismantling the whorearchy and creating therapeutic spaces of safety, restoration, and empowerment for our clients in the sex industry.

Second: How Do We Check Our Biases?

So, now that we know how biases might show up in our mental health work with sex workers . . . what do we do with them? One of the most important things to do is to find someone that you trust with whom you can explore the biases. Where are the biases coming from, and what is it about this particular clinical situation that is allowing these biases to emerge? As in the experience of Padma, sometimes these helpful individuals may come from outside of our immediate work environment. As authors and clinicians, we both belong to professional organizations and communities that continuously provide us with nourishing relationships for such exploration of our biases and viewpoints about a wide range of sexuality-related topics, and an environment in which to process that impact of our therapy provision, and exchange resources. Many of these relationships are not with people with whom we work every day, but they are other professionals whom we can call and say, "I'm feeling a certain way..." Not only have we been this support system for each other, but we have formally asked people we have worked with if they could enter into these spaces with us. Find these sex-positive individuals with whom you can be boldly authentic, and nurture the relationship over time. Even the strongest of these relationships will need tending, especially as your biases and relationships to clinical work will change and grow.

If you do not have such relationships, consider finding a new professional organization or sex-positive community to join in which you can cultivate these types of colleagues. For example, mental health advocacy groups such as certain subgroups of the National Alliance on Mental Illness (NAMI) or the Association of Counseling Sexology and Sexual Wellness can provide helpful information, resources, and a community for clinicians who are wanting to connect with other practitioners with shared values. Other times, colleagues who can support us in bias exploration are not themselves mental health clinicians but can provide nonjudgmental and empathic care. Organizations like Pineapple Support and the Cupcake Girls (two of our respective favorites) can provide us with the types of community that we need both to support us in bias exploration and also to hold us accountable for working through our bias and turning it into competent and informed action.

Outside of these consultations, there are lots of opportunities for understanding our own biases. Continuing education is a great opportunity to create a space for such reflection on and identification of our own biases. One type in particular is Sexual Attitude Reassessments, or SARs. A *SAR* is a process-oriented seminar that uses lecture, media, experiential methods, activities, and small group discussions. Participants in a SAR explore their attitudes, values, feelings, and beliefs about sexual attitudes, behaviors, and identities. SARs also give participants the opportunity to explore how these various topics impact the participants' professional interactions.[21] Unlike traditional classroom settings or continuing education experiences, a SAR does not have traditional learning of content. Instead, a leader of a SAR facilitates a psychoeducational experience that is a highly personal, internal exploration that will be different for each participant.[22] Locally run or virtual SARs could be supportive. However, we strongly suggest attending SARs that emphasize reproductive justice, up-to-date examples of diversity and intersectionality, and how a clinician's erotophobia may intersect with their cultural privilege in one or more areas (e.g., White privilege).

Outside of a SAR, there are multiple additional ways to receive continuing education that can provide opportunities for exploration of biases. A clinician's engagement in professional organizations can often be a source of needed knowledge. We believe that continuing education can (and needs to) come from unlikely sources—some of which happen outside of organizations that are dedicated to mental health. We strongly recommend (actually, we can't recommend strongly enough) that you engage in trainings, speeches, rallies, panel discussions, or public conversations facilitated by and/or featuring current or former sex workers about their experiences and the local political context with which sex workers engage in your local community. As you begin to find the educational spaces that are right for you, having your own set of criteria to evaluate which trainings are worth your time and resources (and which are not) is crucial. Further, finding sex-worker-driven organizations and utilizing social media to find and/or follow informed people who are speaking about sexuality-related cases can also provide additional, needed spaces.

Third: Keep Checking Them.
Again and Again.

....

With this initial recognition of her biases, Padma realizes that she might need to do some further reflection. She first decides to attend a local SAR that is being held by a member of the sex-work community in East Tulsa. As she is a bit nervous about attending the SAR by herself, Padma asks Sue Ellen to go with her. Through a series of experiential activities during the SAR, Padma is able to recognize different facets of her bias about sex work, many of which are connected with some of her internalized classism and media portrayals of sex work as dangerous. As she and Sue Ellen talk after the SAR, Padma discloses to her colleague about her work with Miriam. Sue Ellen is supportive, and suggests that Padma begin to work through some of the obstacles to her clinical work.

After the SAR, Padma first identifies a consultant outside of her agency whom she hires for two consultation sessions. The consultant, a licensed sex therapist whose name was provided at the SAR, helps Padma to identify several podcasts and websites that Padma can use throughout her journey. The consultant also addresses techniques that Padma can use while in session with Miriam both to help regulate herself and to continue to stay present with Miriam when Miriam might feel uncomfortable. Padma also decides to join a virtual sex-positive consultation group, occurring monthly, with professionals across the United States. She speaks with the group's facilitator and explains her reasons for joining, and the facilitator enthusiastically lets her know that the group would be a good fit for her. Padma also begins to listen to a podcast hosted by two different sex workers who speak about their experiences in the industry. She is particularly struck by the hosts' experiences with their doctors, and one of the hosts speaks openly about her own work in therapy. Padma also creates a small sign in her agency's break room with a list of resources on it for other people in her agency to review. She hopes that this sign will help other people in her agency who may not yet have the strength to come forward to do their own internal work in a more private setting.

....

Once you have some understanding of the biases that you do have, you can begin to work on dismantling these biases. Once these biases have made themselves known through consultation or through a SAR, it's time to figure out what to do with them. The first and most important thing is to consult. *"But, you told us to consult earlier. Are you saying that we need to consult again?"* The short answer is *yes*. Talking about these biases with other licensed professionals once you know of their existence achieves two very important goals. One is that talking with others destigmatizes the process of knowing your biases, which will be helpful in eroding many of the systemic problems that we identified earlier in this chapter. Second, the odds are that your colleagues may have ideas about how to work through some of your biases. Specifically, they may know what blogs you should read. Podcasts you should listen to. Articles you should read. The odds are that some of you reading these very words are reading them because a colleague referred you to our work.

A reminder that consultation can be formal or informal. Formal consultation could be an ongoing arrangement that you have with another licensed clinician who has competence and/or expertise in one or more areas related to sex work or sexuality. It can happen individually (one consultant, one clinician) or in a group consultation (one consultant, multiple clinicians). There is lots of literature that speaks to how consultation groups are instrumental in helping clinicians to uncover biases in a supportive environment.[23] Informal consultation could be checking in with a clinician you trust, or creating bonds with clinicians for support or resources. Inherent in consultation is the ingredient of vulnerability and courage with others. What is the most important in all kinds of bias-related consultation is that we use our vulnerability as a tool to help us grow and move forward.

For those of you reading who are not yet licensed (anywhere from starting your first practicum or internship to being days away from taking one of your final licensure exams), clinical supervision is the space to process your biases. Like consultation, it can happen individually (one supervisor, one clinician) or in a group consultation (one supervisor, multiple clinicians).[24] Growing one's skills as a clinician includes knowing who we are and knowing we have certain biases. If you recognize these biases as a pre-licensed clinician, welcome to the process that will repeat itself throughout your career. You are one step closer to more intimately knowing yourself as a healer—including the potential roadblocks that might hinder the healing process that you are providing for clients.

Next, it's important to start exposing your biases to some alternative information. The appendix at the back of this book has a series of resources—books, research articles, podcasts, websites, and blogs—to help you learn more about different aspects of sex workers' experiences and communities. These resources are by no means exhaustive, and we hope that they lead you to other resources that are not on the list. We each find new resources constantly that are continuously challenging our own biases about sex work and about our own areas of needed growth. We hope that you'll eventually create your own list (and share it with the colleagues who will eventually come to you for consultation about their own erotophobia and biases about sex work).

Once you have focused on your attitudinal and cognitive shifting via consultation and your own research, it's time to focus on some behavior. An important part of working with our bias is turning that bias into action and becoming an advocate. The difficult fact for many clinicians is that we are not taught how to be advocates; in fact, advocacy is often left out of the training programs for many therapists.[25] However, the need to do such advocacy is such a paramount part of our work and can reflect the behavior change that we need to do as we own our own biases. What might such bias-focused advocacy look like? One example is the creation of clinically sex-positive/whore-positive spaces in which you are increasing the appreciation of and advocacy for sex workers in your work space. Start a book club, invite a speaker, or have a moment of reflection at the beginning of your staff meeting. Address a whorephobic remark at work by gently commenting, *"I am not sure I agree with that sentiment. I wonder if another way to look at that idea might be ..."* At larger ecological levels, advocacy may look like writing letters to local or national officials about their legislation related to sex work. Chapter 2 of this text defined different forms of legislation that apply to sex workers—what might happen if many of us came together to demand more decriminalization in more parts of the globe?

Hopefully, this chapter has begun to help you reflect upon how we understand the anti-sex-work sentiments that live inside each of us. From small, internalized, fleeting thoughts to large systems of thinking that impact much of who we are as clinicians, we have biases and internalized whorephobia that can impact our clinical practices. Understanding these biases is not only necessary for the safety of our clients, but an ethical mandate that crosses many of our respective professions. As we start to explore these biases, learning where each of us has internalized such discriminatory and oppressive ideas and practices is an important place to start. We all have them, and such feelings include defensiveness, shame, and guilt. Once we uncover them, we need to investigate them more comprehensively. Having a colleague consult with us or attending an experiential workshop with a trained facilitator can ensure that we are receiving the support we need to move past our discomfort and examine the parts of these negative feelings. Finally, we do something about them by educating ourselves and committing to a lifelong shifting of our professional attitudes and behaviors. These steps are just the first ones that we need to take to shift our practice to be more affirming of our clients who work in the sex industry. As we work on our biases, we may begin to realize that other areas of our practice—such as our assessment practices, case conceptualizations, and treatment plans—also need work. Let's look at those next.

RESOURCE 4.1:
Self-Examination of My History with Whorephobia

Messages about sex work and the exchange of sex for money come to us from a variety of sources. Here's an activity to help you reflect on such messages:

1. Make a list of the five to ten messages that you received about sex work before you turned age twenty-one, whether all in one period of your life or dispersed throughout different parts of your life as a child, adolescent, and/or adult. Your engagement with these messages can be voluntary (you watched a movie) or involuntary (you saw an image in a store window, or an advertisement popped up on your computer).

2. Make a list of the five to ten messages that you received about sex work after you turned age twenty-one, whether all in one period of your life or dispersed throughout different parts of your life (in your work as a graduate student, in your personal life, at your workplace, etc.). Your engagement with these messages can be voluntary (you heard your boss at work say a very whorephobic comment and did not say anything) or involuntary (you saw an image in a store window, or an advertisement popped up on your computer).

3. Next, write down what you took from the message with which you engaged. What was either the covert or overt messaging that you received when engaging with this stimuli?

4. In addition to the messages connected with each image, write down one reaction you had (or still have) to the message.

5. As you reflect on these messages, think about the ways in which sex work affects you specifically. Identify two specific themes in your answers.

5

ASSESSMENTS AND ESTABLISHING CONNECTION

....

Aysha identifies as a thirty-one-year-old, biracial (Black and White), cisgender, queer woman who wants to begin therapy services in Raleigh, North Carolina. Although she has sought therapy two times before, she is feeling that she is at a point where, if she does not get some support, things will begin to get "way worse." Aysha has been engaged in various forms of sex work for the past twelve years. She began doing sex work originally to help her pay for school, as she was on her own, unable to afford many of her educational fees, and began working a few nights per week at a strip club to help her pay some expenses. After she completed college with a degree in fine arts and communications, Aysha continued to work in strip clubs, gradually increasing her work to four or five nights per week. She thought about looking for a job in advertising, as Aysha has goals of becoming a graphic designer. She does not know, however, if she wants to give up her lucrative income and work an entry-level job, where she would have to take a significant pay cut and no longer be able to make her own hours. Additionally, Aysha began doing full-service sex work for several of her regular customers outside the strip club. Recently, two of these regulars engaged in violence when she worked with them, resulting in several medical bills and missed days of work. Aysha began drifting further away from several of her clos-est relationships, including friends she had known for a long time. They did not know about Aysha's work as a full-service sex worker, and she did not know if they would approve of her work or judge her. Aysha decided to seek psychotherapy services. As Aysha enters her first therapy appointment, her clinician, Leilani, begins to conduct an initial assessment.

What Is Assessment?

NOW THAT YOU HAVE spent a little time reviewing some of your own biases regarding sex work, let's begin to look at some of the different components of mental health treatment and apply the knowledge learned from the first four chapters of this book. One of the key and instrumental phases of mental health work is the assessment phase. Assessment is one of the most critical but, we would assert, also one of the most overlooked aspects of providing quality mental health care. Assessment is defined as the process of collecting and making interpretations of a client's information. It often involves using interviews to gather this information, but can also occur through observation and testing (cognitive, personality, neuropsychological).[1] Such assessments take several forms, including intake interviews (we call these initial assessments) and also more structured assessments to help with more comprehensive understandings of a client's emotional, cognitive, personality, or neuropsychological functioning. We will focus on intake interviews in this chapter, as other types of testing are helpful but outside the scope of work for some clinicians who may be reading this chapter.

The initial assessment is often the first interaction that occurs between the client and the clinician. When thinking about conducting an initial assessment, we separate assessments into two parts. The first is the *assessment phase* of mental health work. In this initial phase of most clinical work, a clinician builds rapport with the client(s), as well as engages in in-depth exploration about what is happening for the client(s) through the use of (ideally open-ended) questions. During this phase (which could be ten minutes, several hours, or in small five-minute segments over a month—this phase ranges in time!), clinicians will develop and discern what treatment plan is suited for the client(s), begin to collaborate with the client(s) on goal setting, and think about subsequent phases of treatment. The second part of assessments is the *written assessment* itself. This part includes an actual written document (such as an intake form that a client completes) or an initial assessment report that includes information from an intake form synthesized with data gathered from the interview with the clinician. Initial assessments can vary depending on the type of setting in which one works, resulting in some initial assessments occurring within one fifty-minute session, others taking several sessions (e.g., two to three fifty-minute sessions). For mental health workers working outside the parameters of traditional psychotherapy, assessment can also vary greatly, such as a social worker working in a group home for adult women who collects bits of information throughout a seven-day period after a new client arrives at the facility. Variance can also occur in the amount of structure within an initial assessment, as some mental health workers use a structured assessment protocol that includes a list of predetermined questions that are asked in a specific order, whereas other clinicians may have several prompts that guide their initial assessment but will also use client responses to guide and predict follow-up questions.

Although many clinicians know that an initial assessment is important, as well as believe that it is absolutely an essential part of providing a base-line standard of care, many clinicians do not conduct such an assessment process.[2] Reasons for such a lack of assessment are many, including time constraints, not knowing how to do an effective assessment, and/or pressure to move faster into the work with clients. With these constraints, we lose track of the opportunity a good assessment phase can offer the clinician as well as the enhanced support it can provide the client. Further, when working with clients in the sex industry, we can lose the ability to use the initial assessment to create stronger rapport; given the oppressive paradigm and some sex workers' understandable suspicion of the health care industry, the lack of an initial assessment can result in weak rapport. In other mental health work, as our clinical skills grow and our confidence solidifies, we can inadvertently begin to take shortcuts to move deeper into the work at a faster pace. The end result is that we leave behind some of our essential and necessary tools for doing good clinical work—again, resulting in poor rapport with a population of clients who are often already understandably skeptical and cautious.

All of these reasons for a lack of clinical assessment are reasonable and yet can leave both the clinician and the client(s) without a solid foundation on which to do effective clinical work. For example, in the case of Aysha above, we may miss important health information (such as whether she chose to go to the hospital due to her experiences with her clients or what happened subsequently), overlook an opportunity to identify potential supports, or misidentify potential obstacles to treatment. Further, if we're not careful about the assessments that we conduct or the shortcuts we take that result in a limited assessment process, it's very easy to slip into an oppressive paradigm (review chapter 3 for more on this paradigm and how it insidiously switches on during clinical work) that perpetuates harm to our clients. By not gathering adequate clinical information that is bolstered by a strong relationship, we can very easily begin filling in the gaps of clients' stories with our bias and preconceived judgments. By doing what we may believe is a standard assessment, we may not illuminate clients' specific supports or constraints that come with the occupation of sex work.

We believe that the essential point of an assessment is to collect the highest-quality information from a client that enables us to be informed enough to best support the client by reducing distress and suffering and advancing their goals. We can use the initial assessment phase as an opportunity to demonstrate empathy, care, and respect, and to model collaboration with the client every step of the way. If we as clinicians do not actively pursue pro-relational practices, the oppressive paradigm lens will inform the relationship with our client instead. In turn, such a paradigm will interfere with, if not absolutely destroy, the possibility of a healthy and useful therapeutic relationship. Thus, this chapter is dedicated to improving the assessment phase and the resulting assessment documents in our practice with sex workers. As we discuss helpful strategies to improve assessment processes with clients in the sex industry, we will build upon the therapy of Aysha, whom we introduced to you at the beginning of this chapter. Aysha is a composite of clients from both of us, a figure that exemplifies core themes that both of us have seen in our work across many years in facilitating psychological services with sex workers.

Step Away from the Paradigm

....

In her work with Aysha, Leilani begins by welcoming Aysha to her office. Leilani, a licensed professional counselor with expertise in clinical mental health counseling, works in a small community mental health center in the city of Raleigh. Originally from Hawaii, Leilani is a cisgender, Pacific Islander female who has worked in this community mental health center for the last five years. She works predominantly with clients of color and works with individuals who have a variety of presenting concerns and problems. Leilani begins her initial assessment by asking if Aysha had been to therapy before and is familiar with the initial assessment process. Aysha replies that she had been to therapy twice before. In her first attempt, Aysha reports that her previous therapist (an older White, cisgender man) shifted uncomfortably when Aysha disclosed to him in their first session that she worked at a strip club. Throughout the session, Aysha recollects that he would interrupt her and ask if she had ever thought of leaving her "life as a call girl." Aysha had never gone back.

Aysha tells Leilani that, in Aysha's second attempt at therapy, she saw another therapist—a Black woman whom Aysha had guessed was in her mid-fifties—for three sessions. In their first two sessions, Aysha felt seen and heard as she described her experiences of racism and sexism in her previous educational institution, as well as in her work at the strip club. During their third session, the therapist had asked Aysha about growing up as a Black woman. As Aysha had begun to talk about how she understood her identities, the therapist had said to her, "How do you think your work as a sex worker might embody your own racism and sexism?" Startled, Aysha had asked the therapist to explain the question. The therapist had responded, "I wonder what type of hatred you have for yourself if you do not respect yourself enough to let only those you love engage sexually with your body." Although Aysha had stayed for the rest of that session, she reports to Leilani that she knew she would not return. Leilani listens quietly, and when Aysha is done, apologizes for all that had happened with previous experiences and thanks Aysha for being open with her. As the first session between Leilani and Aysha ends, Leilani knows that she will need some consultation, as she had not worked with a client in the sex industry before who had undergone these horrible experiences in therapy.

....

Significant work has been done regarding the positive impact of initial assessment work that is grounded in theoretical treatment modalities such as cognitive behavioral therapy or psychodynamic theory.[3] However, even when a clinician's assessment is grounded in such theory, oppressive or paternalistic paradigms can leak into the process. Such oppressive paradigms are transtheoretical and do not specifically accompany one specific theoretical orientation. Rather, these paradigms can inhabit most theoretical frameworks, which can in turn damage almost any initial assessment. For example, one impact of the oppressive paradigm on initial assessments is the hierarchical ways in which it causes the clinician to think and interact. These ways are embedded in our initial training and in our systems of mental health service provision. It takes consistent, concerted practice and support to move away from these unhelpful and unhealthy paradigms and continue to integrate more relational ways of engaging with our clients.

> *How is that care going to re-traumatize someone . . . if my experience with that psychiatrist who wanted to . . . go through this heavy intake was that, this is traumatizing me, like, you're bullying me, that I'm telling you information around my cognition, because I am a forty-seven-year-old woman who has short-term memory loss and processing delay, and sometimes I can't remember what this is called, like, . . . I'm trying to tell you to respect that. I shouldn't have to re-traumatize myself in order to access the care that I need. People need to be able to access competent care that identifies, but also separates, the preexisting trauma or diagnoses from the [sex] work.*
>
> —SINNAMON

When we conduct an initial assessment with a client who works in the sex industry, we urge you: *Step away from the paradigm.* As is noted in the comment above by one of our consultants, Sinnamon, the oppressive paradigm has locked mental health workers into seeing sex workers in a very specific way through a lens of problems and with the ultimate goal of getting their clients out of the industry. Instead, using a flexible series of questions that can be molded to fit the client's needs in an effective, relational manner will help to establish the beginnings of a trusting relationship for mental health work and can be an intervention by itself. All too often, both of us have heard from our clients who engage or have engaged in sex work that they have tried psychotherapy before, often more than once. As Aysha noted in the vignette above, there are countless times when sex workers enter mental health treatment and have been discriminated against, have been spoken to in a paternalizing, condescending manner, and/or have had their lived experience and resilience overlooked. Further, clinicians will overlook critical concepts of oppression, marginalization, and intersectionality (as you read about in chapter 1) and instead assume that the client is there to be "saved" from the sex industry. When you begin working with client(s) who have been or are a sex worker, you will (as we have many times) have the work of acknowledging and cleaning up the harmful encounters with and ruptures from previous clinicians while creating space to affirm fear and/or anger from the client toward the mental health system.

Scaffolding an Effective Assessment Process

As you begin to develop trust and heal previous experiences with your client in the sex industry, we also encourage you to scaffold the initial assessment process. You may remember the term *scaffold* from your child development courses or from education training that some of you may have received. Scaffold refers to a method of supporting someone as they learn and develop a new concept or skill.[4] More specifically, when applied to clinical work, clinicians can explicitly support their clients in the sex industry to know what to expect in an initial assessment (including how the assessment may differ from subsequent phases of mental health treatment).

We have found that, when working with our clients who do sex work, care, communication, and collaboration go a long way to establish rapport, cultivate trust, and maintain a therapeutic relationship throughout the psychotherapy process. We will discuss specifically what we mean by these three words. By *care,* we specifically mean that we urge clinicians to be mindful of their tone of voice, eye contact, and word choice and to find ways that demonstrate that the clinician is engaging in a thoughtful manner. By *communication,* we mean practicing transparency (i.e., informing a client *why* you are asking for a particular piece of information, or laying out your thought process for a decision or an interpretation you have arrived at). Additionally, ask the client for consent to continue with a particular line of questions and explicitly state why you are asking, and offer the client the opportunity to consent or decline to answer questions then or in the future. By *collaboration,* we mean coming to a shared agreement about the client's goals and how to manage treatment, explicitly soliciting input and feedback from the client about how they are perceiving the therapeutic process, and actively leveraging the client's intelligence and resourcefulness, among other practices.

There are several elements that a therapist can gather to assist them in creating a conducive therapy environment for good-quality assessments. We would assert that one of the things is often overlooked: you. The clinician being as relaxed and embodied as possible is important and matters for many reasons. One critical reason is that how you feel *does matter* in the room, as your tension or relaxation is communicated to the client. It's important to make sure that you are comfortable, and that you have what you need, so that you are as fully present as possible and can offer a clinically supportive environment for your client. Whether doing telehealth sessions or in-person sessions, these general invitations are the same for either type of session. We invite you to have water, tea, or coffee and invite the client to have something as well. This can be very relaxing and inviting. By creating a welcoming and gentle environment for you and for the client, you are setting the tone for developing a thorough assessment, modeling self-care and care for others, and pushing back against the kind of rigid or sterile frame that too many people experience when interacting with health care providers.

Assessment Forms and Initial Paperwork

Many mental health workers have new clients and consumers with whom they work complete some necessary paperwork. As you begin the assessment phase, your assessment paperwork can be digital, or you can create a hard copy. We recommend that you be thoughtful and transparent about what is in your assessment paperwork, as the wording that you choose in your paperwork can communicate a lot to your clients about you and your comfort levels before the client ever meets with you (for specific ways that your biases might enter your wording on forms, we encourage you to revisit chapter 4). We encourage you to think about wording that you use that might indicate openness to clients' multiple partners, clients having partners of different sexes and genders, and clients being able to identify with multiple categories with regard to their sociocultural identities (e.g., clients having multiple ethnicities, occupations, jobs, etc.). One of our close colleagues loves to tell the story of the day that she realized that her intake paperwork asked the respondent to write about "a job" or "an occupation," and that the minute she made these words plural (i.e., jobs, occupations), she learned a lot more about clients.

Being transparent about not only intake paperwork but also questions that you might ask during an interview can help to build trust with clients. It can also relieve stress on clients to give them all assessment paperwork beforehand so they can see some of the questions that you will be asking them. Another option can occur in session: You can have a list of questions in front of you that you want to ask and concurrently also give the client a copy of the same questions. Such transparency allows clients to review your questions and read along with you. Such transparency can be very helpful for establishing a sense of trust and mutuality. If you are a clinician who does not like to use lists of questions, a third option is to keep in mind the assessment questions that you want to ask and then gently weave those into your session time with the client.

When it comes to your assessment paperwork, just as with your intake paperwork, pay particular attention to create forms or other avenues of contact that are accessible and inviting, whether it's an online form, an in-person form, or contact by phone or video conferencing. The language used in your intake should be inviting and helpful and should take their world into account. For example, this could mean having a variety of choices for gender. If you do ask for occupation, you can list not just sex work but you can list different types or kinds of sex work. You can give them options asking them what name they prefer to use. Some clients are going to want to use their stage/professional name; other clients are going to want to use their legal names or another name that's very meaningful to them. When you can, mindfully create space in your assessment to ask these questions. Another idea is to make sure that you're being very clear about gender and gender options and sexual orientation; and if the client states that in their performing life they express their gender one way or come across as one gender one way but their actual gender or pronouns are something else, it's critical to honor that in your paperwork and any communications with the client. These ideas should be baseline for any client, but particularly for this population, honoring the language that they use to describe their situation is critical. If you make a mistake along any of these lines and the client has the courage to tell you about it, immediately apologize, make the change, or let them know when the change will be made. Your word is critical.

From your outward-facing materials, to initial contact, to your assessment and beyond, a therapeutic process with sex workers is supported by transparency, checking in with the client, allowing for privacy and trust to be built, suspending judgment, and maintaining curiosity.

The Intake Interview

Once your client has received paperwork and you have a sense of what to ask, it's time to move forward in your assessment phase and conduct a clinical interview. In framing the interview, we encourage you to be especially transparent in the first three or four sessions, given the difficulty that many sex workers have had with various health care providers. One example of such framing is:

> *"I'm going to be doing an assessment with you now. The purpose of the assessment is to get an idea about who you are and what is happening with you. The more information I have, the better help that I can provide for you. However, please feel free to ask me any questions about this process, and please know that you do not have to answer these questions right now. You can always answer them later, or you don't have to answer them at all if you don't feel comfortable."*

During the assessment phase, we strongly encourage you to continue to model slowing down, intentionality, and finding opportunities to invite the client into the process with you.

The overall questions that you ask in a clinical interview may vary depending on your place of work, your theoretical orientation, and your style. Additionally, although it may seem awkward to ask questions about substance use (prescribed or not) or violence or a history of feeling unsafe or self-harm, it's important to move in toward the awkwardness or discomfort. Any of these topics are delicate and can feel very loaded, but it's also critically important to model clear, stigma-free communication with your clients in the sex industry, to get a clear picture of how your client is functioning currently, and to track what they've been doing in the recent past (and sometimes even further back) if you feel as if that's needed. As we've noted, conducting a good assessment phase is about engaging in a clinical interview in which the client feels comfortable enough to share an accurate-enough picture of their world.

Resource 5.1 has some specific questions that we ask our clients in the sex industry that we usually add into our respective traditional series of assessment questions. Notice that, although the resource introduces these questions in a list format, it might be helpful to consider the order in which you ask the questions, or co-constructing the introduction of these questions with the clients whom you serve. As you think about your own intake interview and practices that you conduct in your own assessment phases, below are seven key tips and strategies that we think will be helpful along your journey:

1. **Frame your work.** As you start your assessment phase, we encourage you to develop a short introduction (that you speak at the beginning of your intake interview) on how and why you choose to work with the sex-worker population. Practice this introduction so that you feel comfortable with it and so that you can feel good about how it exemplifies your values.

2. **Scaffold questions and answers.** Allow your clients to know what they should expect in their intake. Use framing interventions such as: *"Today is going to feel a bit different from other phases of our*

work together. I'm going to ask you a series of questions, and it may feel more like an interview than a conversation. Also, after any question that I ask, you can tell me you do not want to answer. You can also ask me, 'Why are you asking me that?'" Such experiences allow sex workers more ability to co-construct their therapeutic process.

3. **Let's (explicitly) talk about sex.** Do not forget that clients in the sex industry will be looking for clues that you are sex positive—especially if they have had erotophobic and whorephobic interactions and experiences with other health care providers. Being explicit about your relationship to sexuality as a mental health worker (*"I want you to know that it's okay for us to talk about sex if you want to. We can talk about sex today, or in future sessions when you might want to bring it up or feel more comfortable"*) can often result in your clients in the sex industry walking away from an initial assessment feeling confident that they will be able to come back and disclose more information. We have heard hundreds of stories of sex workers who go back to therapy, and three, four, or five sessions after the initial assessment say to their clinician, *"Remember when you said we could talk about sex any time? Well, I was thinking ..."*

4. **Allow sex (work) to be one topic among many.** Do not focus all your assessment questions on the subject of sex and/or the occupation of sex work. Your clients in the sex industry are whole people with lots of different facets to who they are (like all of your clients). Unless their work in the sex industry is a main part of what they want to address in their mental health treatment, it is important that clinicians follow the client's lead about how much clients want to address their participation in the industry. In addition, clinicians should be open to various themes and topics that sex workers bring in that have no connection to their participation in the industry (and, as the clinician, don't force connections).

5. **Notice nonverbal cues about certain topics.** We encourage you to follow the client's lead when it comes to what they want to speak about during sessions. If clients want to share information, we need to move toward that desire and speak with them about what they've shared. Likewise, if clients do not want to share about certain topics,

we need to take the hint. As current literature indicates, it is important for us to ask when there is a need, as clients will often not know if it is safe to disclose information unless we ask. However, if we ask, we also need to respect the responses, including "I don't want to talk about that today."

6. **Don't push for details or deep disclosures.** We have heard about some mental health workers who ask sex workers repeatedly in their initial assessments about sex work, despite sex workers indicating verbally and/or nonverbally that they don't want to speak about their work. Some clinicians hear that boundary as a challenge, re-forming or rephrasing questions to see if they can get at some information. *Such pushing against boundaries can be very dangerous.* As you read about in earlier sections of this book, many sex workers have experienced violence, discrimination, and a complete disregard for their boundaries by law enforcement, social service providers, and various macro-level institutions. When conducted with care and competence, the assessment phase is an opportunity for you to begin to heal and correct your client's experiences.

7. **Optional, but not required.** As clients in the industry begin to feel safe, they may share more information with mental health workers with whom they are connected. We encourage you to invite sharing of further information but to not make it a requirement of your work. Further, if clients do not share certain information, avoid an assumption that the client is "resistant" if they don't go deep into details of their work, family, or other potentially sensitive topics. Sex workers' developing trust with systems and organizations that have harmed them can be difficult, and we need to respect their autonomy and whatever time it takes to move to another level of trust.

Once the initial assessment phase begins to end and you feel as though you have all of the data that you need to move forward with the work (again, an assessment phase can be anywhere from one session to several sessions depending on the theoretical orientation, work environment, etc.), you can begin to assess the outcomes of your assessment phase. If you've done a good assessment with a client, ideally you feel that you have a good idea about their current level of functioning—emotionally, physically, sexually, and legally (especially if there have been difficult incidents with law enforcement, etc.). Additionally, it's extremely helpful if you have clarity about their current social and occupational supports and current stressors or troubles, and are able to sum up their presenting concern(s), their reason for coming to see you, any goals that they have for their own treatment, any current challenges or crises that they're in the middle of, and their perceived current level of physical, emotional, occupational, and financial safety, and sexual health. If you have enough information to do something to support them both immediately as well as in the medium term and long term, such information is a good indication that you have something to build on as you continue doing work with a client (we will review more information on short-term and long-term goal setting with clients in the sex industry in chapter 7).

Writing in the Assessment Phase: Moving from the Interview to the Page

After getting some consultation from a colleague who had expertise in mental health practice with sex workers, Leilani starts her clinical interview by providing an overview of the intake process. Leilani begins her overview by disclosing her own philosophy of sex positivity to Aysha, letting Aysha know explicitly what she believes about sex-worker rights. She discloses that she and Aysha can talk about sex today or whenever Aysha feels comfortable in their relationship. Leilani also begins by orienting Aysha to the process of her intake style, letting her know that, even though Aysha had been to therapy before, Leilani will ask a series of questions that may be different from the questions asked by other providers with whom Aysha had worked. Leilani hands Aysha a written series of questions that she often asks individuals who work in the sex industry. She then asks Aysha a series of questions about her functioning. Leilani then asks if Aysha feels comfortable if she asks Aysha some questions from the list that Aysha had reviewed about her job as a sex worker to learn more about Aysha's experiences. Aysha replies that she feels comfortable. They then engage in a conversation about Aysha's experiences of safety. After two sessions of gathering information, Leilani feels as though she has sufficient information to write her intake report. She is hesitant, however, to write the report, as she is uneasy about including some information about Aysha's work that might be attached to her medical record ...

....

As clinicians complete their clinical interview and complete their assessment phase, they usually complete some sort of written intake report (sometimes called an initial assessment report). Different organizations have different formats for these reports, but they usually have common elements, including a synthesis of information about multiple domains of client functioning and a mental health diagnosis from the *Diagnostic and Statistical Manual of Mental Disorders,* 5th edition, text revision *(DSM-5-TR).*[5]

In chapter 3, we wrote about the multiple ways that the oppressive paradigm has resulted in clinicians providing inaccurate, biased diagnoses of individuals in the sex industry. Let us not mince words: *The process and outcome of your diagnosis of the client has an opportunity to break the cycle of the oppressive paradigm.* Of course, if you have a client who is in the sex industry who has undergone severe trauma in their childhood, then of course provide an accurate diagnosis that reflects that trauma that you will work with in treatment. However, we encourage you to question whether a diagnosis you would assign a client in the sex industry is because of the client's prior experiences, or the client's labor as a sex worker. As you reflect on this encouragement, you may connect your thoughts to some of our writings about biases in chapter 4 (and with good reason). As there is rampant bias in the diagnosis of mental health symptoms, we encourage you to reflect on these biases and inquire as to whether they are taking part in your initial assessments with clients in the sex industry and how such bias might be occurring.

As you write your assessment report, we hope that you might have questions similar to Leilani's in the vignette above. Specifically, what is information that you want to include in an intake report? Our rule is that we do not put information into the report that we do not want other people to see. If you believe there is a good chance that a client may be involved in a legal proceeding (e.g., a difficult divorce, a custody battle over children, or some sort of concern with employment discrimination at a job), proceed with caution about including previous or current involvement in the sex industry. Although we wish that all individuals involved in such legal proceedings were sex positive, we both have heard many unfortunate stories that have resulted in our knowing that such is not the case. It is also important to ensure that you have a conversation with your client(s) in the sex industry about what information related to their job status they feel comfortable having documented. In addition, clients may prefer your using more general language (e.g., "altercation at work" instead of "fight with the police at a brothel") to describe job-related incidents or stress that you feel compelled to document. Co-constructing the boundaries related to written initial assessments is crucial in creating a space where clients feel safe and trust your documentation process as a baseline to engage in subsequent phases of treatment.

As you've read in this chapter, it is crucial that your assessment process reflect your stance as both sex positive and sex-worker-affirming. Creating an initial space that is welcoming for sex workers who are attempting to connect with a mental health provider can be the difference between a client who continues treatment and a client who has several awful encounters with a provider and never goes back (even though that person may need supportive mental health treatment!). Integrating your knowledge about language and historical trends of the oppressive paradigm can ensure that you do not replicate harm in your mental health practice to communities of sex workers who need affirmative and supportive treatment. We encourage you to think about how both parts of the assessment process—the assessment phase and the written assessment itself—can be insidiously connected to whorephobia in many different ways.

As you move through the assessment phase—from forms to questions to the interview process to writing an assessment report—we encourage you to reflect back on our three key words: care, communication, and collaboration. Further, we encourage you to be explicit about your sex positivity in all aspects of the assessment process. These guiding principles will be an important part of your work to ensure that your clients in the industry feel supported, and will provide them hope that treatment can be effective. With that hope, clients in the sex industry will begin to see the value of mental health treatment, and they will come back to see you. As you move out of the assessment phase, let's now review later phases of your work with clients who are sex workers, including case conceptualization and treatment planning.

RESOURCE 5.1:
Assessment Tool with Sex-Worker Clients

The following questions can be added onto (or incorporated into) an initial intake assessment. Some clinicians prefer to ask these questions during an initial session. Other clinicians weave these questions in gradually to various sessions during the assessment phase.

1. What type(s) of work do you do (e.g., full service, camming, porn acting, etc.)?
2. In what type of setting do you work (e.g., independent fee-for-service, brothel, club, group practice, etc.)?
3. How long have you been in the industry?
4. How is it to talk about your work in the industry with me? What would make it easier and/or more comfortable to talk about your work with me?
5. Have you experienced adverse working conditions (e.g., violence with police while at work, violent clients, unsafe working conditions)?

    a. Have these conditions impacted you, if at all?

6. What sources of social support help you navigate difficult situations at work?
7. Do you have colleagues in the industry? In what ways do these colleagues provide you support?
8. How do you take care of yourself?

    a. Exercise?
    b. Health habits?
    c. Mental health habits (including breathing, meditation, and regulation strategies)?

9. What part of working in the industry do you like?
10. What parts of the industry are difficult for you and/or do you not like?

6

CONCEPTUALIZING TREATMENT

....

Malik is a twenty-four-year-old, Black American therapist who has just started working in a private practice setting in San Diego, California. Malik graduated from his master's program in social work approximately a year ago, and feels very proud to have been offered a job in a private practice with Dr. Sylvia Sanders, a Black-identified, forty-eight-year-old licensed clinical social worker with a doctorate in social work who has agreed to supervise Malik in her practice so that he can earn the remainder of his needed supervised hours for his own licensure as a licensed clinical social worker. Malik has started to deliver services to three new clients, and meets for weekly clinical supervision with Dr. Sanders for support and guidance on his clinical work.

One of these new clients is Arianne, a twenty-nine-year-old, biracial (Black and White), transgender woman who has come to therapy due to some difficulty in daily functioning. In her intake session with Malik, Arianne reports that she has been having problems sleeping and has been having difficult nightmares that "often result in me waking up in the middle of the night and I can't get back to sleep." She reports not feeling rested and having nightmares three to four times a week. She also reports recently ending her intimate relationship with her boyfriend of three years after she found out that he had been lying to her about being monogamous with her although they had agreed to monogamy. Arianne reports that she attends a master's program in anthropology, and she hopes to soon apply to PhD programs where she would like to study the transgender rights movement. Arianne notes that, given the stress of school, work, and applying to doctoral programs, she has been feeling "more on edge than I usually do . . . and it doesn't help that I'm not sleeping."

Arianne tells Malik that she has been earning some money to help pay for school using OnlyFans, where she posts pictures and videos of herself dancing in different amounts of clothing, including nudity. Malik has not worked with a client who is a sex worker before. After his initial session, he begins to organize information and prepare for the next session . . . but feels a little lost. How much should he focus on Arianne's work as a sex worker? Malik worries that, if he brings up his questions to Dr. Sanders, she will think that he is incompetent.

As we move into the final chapters of the book, it's time to get to some of the most clinical parts of mental health work when working with clients in the sex industry: case conceptualization and treatment. Armed with the knowledge about sex-worker communities from chapters 2 and 3 and some increased awareness of attitudes toward sex work from chapter 4, we are now focusing on clinical skills. In chapter 5, we focused more on considerations and techniques for the initial clinical assessment and those initial meetings with clients. However, you're probably asking, *"Now that the intake assessment is complete . . . what do I do?"* We would like to welcome you to the "next part."

After the clinical intake assessment, many clinicians like Malik in the vignette above engage in a process of organizing the information that they learned in their initial assessment. Additionally, clinicians will add some of their therapeutic knowledge to this organizational process in the forms of diagnoses, cultural context (consider issues of privilege, oppression, and/or marginalization described in chapter 1), and/or psychological theory in order to understand what might be happening for a client. This combination of additional diagnoses and theories can also help clinicians begin to plan the road map of their work with clients in the form of a treatment plan. Scholars have defined the term *case conceptualization* as an organizational strategy in which they cluster information from various domains of a client's life (such as initial symptoms and/or previous functioning in the context of family, relationships, and health) and apply diagnostic and theoretical information to the case to use in their work.[1] When complete, a conceptualization is an organized presentation of information from the intake, often culminating in a diagnosis and some general recommendations for treatment (such as whether specific referrals are needed to providers such as a psychiatrist, a case manager, or a primary care doctor and/or if a client would benefit from individual, group, relationship, or family counseling, etc.). The case conceptualization is connected to but also distinct from a *treatment plan,* which offers a structured series of treatment goals and interventions for the clinician(s) and client(s) to use as a therapeutic "road map."[2]

When we have created a case conceptualization in sexuality-focused clinical work, our experiences have taught us that too often clinicians use diagnoses, theories, and other clinical approaches that inadvertently bring erotophobia into the work (refer back to chapter 4 if you need a refresher on this concept). As we have demonstrated in previous chapters, sex negativity and erotophobia permeate the research, theories, trainings, and clinical practice of mental health workers. If we as mental health providers want to do better by our clients and increase the chances of better mental health outcomes, then we need better elements to create a useful and effective case conceptualization. Specifically, a well-intentioned clinician like Malik working with a client who is a sex worker may make some errors that can result in an inaccurate understanding of what the client might need. Such errors, even if they are driven by good intentions, when formulating our approach to clinical work with sex workers, are avoidable with a well-thought-out case conceptualization that takes a holistic and nonpathologizing view of sex work. For example, let's say Malik and Dr. Sanders choose a one-size-fits-all clinical approach or approaches that are individualistic and erotophobic in focus and locate the client's distress as a personal failing that is linked to the client's job as a sex worker. This individualistic and erotophobic framing erases other potential stressors and ignores that the client's distress may not have anything to do with being a sex worker at all. The following sections will break down different facets of creating a sex-work-positive case conceptualization that supports you in your work.

Two Halves of the Whole, Part 1: Ethics

As you begin to think about your post-intake work with clients who are sex workers, let's first focus in on our ethics as our primary guide. Ethics are our foundation for how we decide how to conduct our professional relationships. Although we wrote a lot about ethics in chapter 4 when we discussed knowing our biases, we want to share about more subtle and less discussed aspects of ethics and how they influence clinical work when conceptualizing cases. Typically, in the field of mental health provision, professors, supervisors, and trainers discuss how important self-awareness is in being thoughtful and ethical. We agree with such statements and also assert that other clinical ethics besides self-awareness play into providing supportive psychotherapy to sex workers (and working with themes of sexuality in clinical work more generally). In a landmark published article, Naomi Meara and colleagues[3] noted the importance of two concurrent types of ethics when working with clients. One type is *principle ethics,* or our "baseline quality control ethics." These principle ethics are the standards that we abide by that are used in the formation of the ethical codes that we apply in the mental health profession. The second type is *virtue ethics,* or our morals and character; these are the values that describe how we choose to engage and live with others. When our various professional ethics codes do not have a specific code that prescribes what to do in a given situation (because no code has all the answers for every situation with which we will come into contact), our virtues help us make decisions based on the values that we hold. When combined, our principle and virtue ethics not only adhere to an official code of ethics, but also help us to identify and tap into our ethical framework. This framework helps us make decisions that support us to do right by clients when there is no clear, correct answer.

When we are working with clients in the sex industry, there are a few principle and virtue ethics that routinely come into our work that are noteworthy. The first is the principle of *nonmaleficence,* or the idea of "do no harm." Chances are that you are aware of the principle of nonmaleficence within the medical context, and it is another shared standard that can provide common ground for mutual understanding and collaboration between the mental health and medical fields. This principle ethic has a direct relationship with the virtue ethics of being prudent, being truthful, and having fidelity. To embody these virtue ethics means to be loyal to and supportive of the welfare of our clients and to be thoughtful in our actions about the ways in which our actions can impact our clients' futures. Specifically, one way that we can practice the idea of "do no harm" as we work through developing a case conceptualization is to be as thorough as possible in understanding all of the information presented in an intake session. Consider all aspects of a client when organizing information—not just the client's employment in the sex industry. Are certain parts of the client's symptoms related to their work in the industry or, for example, are Arianne's symptoms in the vignette above better explained by the breakup of an intimate relationship after finding out about infidelity as well as stress about school and future PhD programs? It is also important to consider nonmaleficence when documenting a case conceptualization or an intake report that could endanger a sex worker. For example, writing information in your notes that is not clinically relevant about a client who is doing sex work could endanger the safety of that client if those notes are reported to the police or subpoenaed in a legal proceeding. Depending on the type of organization you work for and what state you work in, non–clinically relevant information such as Social Security number, a client's sexual orientation, their drug use, citizenship status, or other personal information could result in cutting off a client from certain social services that the client uses to help themselves or their dependents, or even worse eventualities.

Another ethical consideration for clinical work is *competence*. If you are unqualified to work with a client, you may be causing them harm through your counseling. There is not a more gentle way to put it. As noted in chapter 4, getting necessary training on bias awareness is a vital component in increasing competence. However, our sense of competence should not stop there. It is also important to receive ongoing training in evidence-based practices that can be adapted to use with the sex-worker population. One example is trauma-informed care (given the level of societal violence and stigma directed at sex-worker populations), which we will discuss later in this chapter.

One question that we often get asked individually and together is *"How do I know that I am competent to see a client who is a sex worker?"* Although different clinicians, clinical supervisors, and clinical directors will have different responses to this question, we have a very specific stance. In chapter 3, we outlined how the oppressive paradigm has historically led many mental health service providers to believe that any and all providers could work with sex workers and that their goal should be to help their clients leave the industry. In contrast, we strongly feel that not every mental health worker can or should deliver services to clients who are sex workers, and that specific key factors *need* to be present for competent services to take place. One such factor is that, in addition to being a clinician who continually checks their biases, there must be willingness to care in an engaged manner instead of as a "savior." That is, can you be a clinician who genuinely cares for and seeks to collaborate with your clients who are sex workers minus the desire to "save" or "rescue" them from the industry? Another component is attending specific trainings on an ongoing basis focused on social services for sex workers. And finally, the clinician should engage, over time, with sex-worker-led communities (such as rallies, panels, and presentations) virtually and/or in person. It is crucial that clinicians learn from sex workers themselves about sex workers' own mental health needs so that clinicians can actively and effectively dismantle the oppressive paradigm and begin to conceptualize clients through a lens that is sex positive and wellness focused.

Adding to our ethics of nonmaleficence and competence is our third reoccurring ethical consideration that is of particular importance with this population: *confidentiality*. Of course, in almost all situations governed by laws, confidentiality is a critical element for clinicians delivering mental health services. However, the principle of confidentiality is of particular importance in small communities. Scholars have noted the unique challenges of how small communities can create challenges for confidentiality in the context of mental health services.[4] Sex-worker communities tend to be small and very interconnected, especially given that members often provide each other with needed emotional, social, and vocational support given the stress occurring on or related to the job. Thus, a clinician like Malik could be working with two individual clients who are sex workers who are themselves connected in their vocational world. An additional example is that if one therapist is known and trusted to provide therapy to sex workers, they therefore could be working with several clients who are a group of interconnected folks outside of the therapeutic space. Clinicians should strive to ensure that they are only discussing information about the work with one client that they learned only from that client (and not from another client).

One thing my therapist does also that no therapist has ever done before with me is when I share a particularly difficult story, which now I'm so self-conscious about talking about trauma, because of the way I can traumatize other people. I feel even more self-conscious talking about my own life now than I ever have when it comes to those experiences. And this therapist, I'll ask her consent. I'll say, "I'm coming up on a story that has some violence in it. Can I tell it?" She's never said no. Although she always says, "Yes," I think she would say no if she felt like it was going to be too hard for that day. Or if we only have five minutes left, she's going to say "Hold it" and I feel like she would actually say no to hearing the story for that day. It's truly asking and truly giving consent. And then she thanks me, after I've done it, she says, "Thank you for trusting me with that." And it changes the whole framework of power there for me. I'm not asking this person to approve of me or my life; I am asking this person to bear witness. And for them to bear true witness, they have to honor and understand how difficult it is to narrate some of these things, and how I'm doing it in search of movement, and shifting. And she sees that as trust, and she thanks me for the trust, and that has changed it for me; it's made me feel so much safer. I think that an important thing for clinicians to think about is: If you want to work with sex workers, you got to be ready for some of this stuff to come up. If you don't push it, you don't assume it's coming. But when it's gonna come, some of it is hard shit. Some of it is sexual trauma. Some of it is violence. Some of it is drug stuff; some of it is just, you know, the kind of slow trauma of being in a life where people aren't respecting you enough. There's all of this stuff that can come up. I think probably you shouldn't think of yourself as a sex-worker-friendly therapist without understanding that you need to be really deft and nimble with trauma work. You need to know how to do it.

—VANESSA

The above ethical considerations are the start of an excellent foundation from which to work with clients in the sex industry. In addition to nonmaleficence, competence, and confidentiality, there are three other important ethical considerations that have supported us in our work and that we believe are essential when working with this population and when providing sex-positive mental health care in general: courage, creativity and compassion. Sometimes, when we are engaging in therapy with clients (and this may have already happened to you), we hear things that are frightening or disturbing, either that have happened to our clients or in which they have engaged. Additionally, when our colleagues learn that we are providing psychotherapy to sex workers that does not center the goal of "saving" these clients, these colleagues will have judgments about us and the work that we do. It is crucial that we practice maintaining the strength to persevere in sex-positive treatment through difficulty, discouragement, and fear. Courage is not about an absence of feeling challenged or a lack of painful emotions, but instead it is the practice of grounding ourselves in knowledge that we can withstand the stress or adversity in front of us.

Creativity is the fifth of the ethical considerations that we use as a guide in our work as therapists, clinical supervisors, and trainers. Specifically, in doing therapy with clients who engage in sex work, sometimes there can be many factors at play in their lives. Further, there can be federal and state laws that go into effect that can radically impact their lives and cause shifts in income or in income opportunities, housing, mental health, or physical health of themselves or loved ones. Such factors can impact our clients between therapy sessions, so maintaining a stance of creativity and flexibility can help alleviate confusion or frustration and enhance the therapeutic relationship by working with the client to understand what their current situation is. In creativity, you can find how you can be supportive *today* while continuing to gather information to build your case conceptualization and treatment plan that will be supportive in an ongoing manner.

The final ethical consideration that guides our work is compassion—more specifically, compassion for others and compassion for ourselves. As exemplified by Vanessa's story of asking for consent to tell a traumatic story to her therapist and also being thanked by her therapist for disclosing trauma-related material, having a relationship rooted in mutual compassion is critical for clinicians and their clients in the sex industry. For various reasons, both sex work and undergoing mental health treatment can be challenging fields of endeavor and they can take a toll. As clinicians, we are not going to know everything or respond flawlessly to the challenges with which we are confronted, but what we can do is stay aware of our clients' distress and suffering, take thoughtful action with ourselves and our clients, and do what we can.

As you read through the next part of the vignette below, take time to consider how you see these six core ethical considerations that we have discussed being practiced through the supervision that Malik receives from Dr. Sanders. We also urge you to consider how these ethics help him develop his case conceptualization for his work with Arianne.

Two Halves of the Whole, Part 2: Advocacy and Social Justice

....

Malik begins to create a conceptualization for his work with Arianne. He first begins by engaging in some self-reflection related to his biases about sex workers. Malik knows that he has not had much exposure to sex-worker communities. In addition, he also realizes that, apart from several lectures in his graduate program, he has never received information on providing services for a transgender client. As he reflects on Arianne's identities, Malik realizes that he has biases about transgender individuals as well as about people who are sex workers. He decides it is important to bring these thoughts to Dr. Sanders (Sylvia). As he describes his reflections in his next session of clinical supervision, Sylvia listens with curiosity and empathy. She acknowledges that she and Malik live in a country and society where employment discrimination disproportionately impacts sex workers and transgender people, and that these two communities consequently have many similarities in terms of the outcomes of marginalization. She thanks Malik for being open with her. Because Malik has reported that he has struggled with forming a case conceptualization for his work with Arianne, Sylvia suggests that they first use the theoretical framework of social justice and self-advocacy to identify places where Arianne may feel disempowered in her work as a graduate student, as a sex worker, in her relationship (that has recently ended), and as a Black-identified woman in a country plagued by multiple histories of racialized and gendered injustice. Sylvia and Malik also begin to use a lens of intersectionality to identify the points of connection among these various identities that may cause additional stress and stigma for Arianne.

Once information provided by the client has been systematically organized for the purposes of case conceptualization and planning for further stages of your work, it can be helpful to bring in theory and/or diagnosis. Many mental health workers have a theoretical orientation, or a frame through which they view, interpret, and hope to resolve the symptoms and suffering that their clients experience. Typically, clinicians utilize one or more theoretical orientations because the clinician finds that frame a useful model for explaining or navigating human behavior and for helping people. By extension, most clinicians hope that their theoretical orientation will be helpful and meaningful to the clients they serve as well. Various theories of personality, counseling, and psychotherapy have been generated within the field of mental health practice for the last century, resulting in copious writing and fierce debates about the efficacy of one theory over the other and/or comparing which theories work "better" to achieve therapeutic outcomes.[5] However, *regardless* of the other theories that a clinician uses to inform their clinical practice, social justice must be a part of one's clinical lens and integrated into one's clinical practice when working with sex workers.

Multiple disciplines have articulated that advocacy is a metatheoretical concept that can be integrated with and applied to other theories that a clinician chooses to use. That is, advocacy is not a specific theory that should be used only when conceptualizing certain clients; it is instead a sustainable practice that all mental health providers should support their clients to practice and use to remove systemic barriers and promote equity for their clients who are forced to engage with systemic oppression and experiences of marginalization (for a review of these concepts, reread chapter 1 where we outline these concepts in detail). Understanding the unique experiences of stigma, oppression, and marginalization experienced by sex work necessitates that all clinicians serving clients in this community actively engage in advocacy efforts with and on behalf of sex workers. We understand that our perspective may be challenging for some readers and, if you are challenged by our stance, we invite you to contemplate why that may be. The truth is, if one looks at the histories of psychology, personality, and psychotherapy, most theories of psychotherapy and applied psychology have traditionally not included advocacy in their understanding about human functioning.[6, 7, 8]

This historical absence is problematic at best, as the lack of advocacy does not meet the needs of many clients in therapy, particularly those from systemically and historically marginalized communities. Specifically, such lack of advocacy has understandably resulted in some sex workers engaging in adaptive suspicion of mental health service providers and systems where there is no clear evidence of advocacy.[9] To explain further, adaptive suspicion refers to a *reasonable and understandably heightened* cautious, doubting, or mistrustful attitude that individuals and communities may have about care providers. This adaptive suspicion may and can shift or soften when a client begins to feel trust, or when a provider does or says certain things to make people feel comfortable, but a certain level of vigilance and skepticism or wanting to please and "be good" may always remain. Think of a time when you repeatedly have not gotten the services that you wanted from a person or institution and have been treated poorly in the process. You can probably remember somatically/psychologically arming yourself with a resilient hypervigilance that you hoped you would be able to put away but knew might rise up in order to protect yourself from further frustration or harm. Or you may have made yourself seem pleasing, harmless, inoffensive, or hypercompliant. Now imagine if this experience is repeated day after day, year after year, with almost all systems that a modern adult must interface with. If you cannot connect with this experience, again, we urge you to deeply examine why that is.

When we are conceptualizing sex workers as clients, locating our role as advocates for each client is essential. *We need to advocate,* often at different systemic levels. At an individual level, we can advocate for clients in our office when we mirror their words about incidents of violence or their fear of law enforcement officials. We can help them find safe spaces in person or virtually when they feel isolated and need more support. We can also advocate at community levels by ensuring that sex workers have access to resources and safe(er) spaces, and that community watch programs allow sex workers to feel safe going to work, working, and leaving their work environments. Finally, we can advocate at macro levels when we name whorephobia as present in different institutions and dismantle the oppressive paradigm within various disciplines of mental health such as in our master's programs, clinical trainings, practicum sites, etc. These are just some examples, but we can name numerous other opportunities for advocacy for sex-worker communities. If your case conceptualization is to be complete and truly nourishing, advocacy is fundamental.

We Love Theory, But ...

Now that our efforts as advocates and change agents are under way, let's discuss specific theories as they pertain to our case conceptualization. Why is it important to examine theory? Because, unfortunately, throughout the history of psychotherapy, certain fundamental assumptions about "normal" versus "deviant" sexuality, constructs about race, gender, and class, about what it means to be a "productive" member of society, were woven into theoretical modalities that have had profoundly harmful impacts on marginalized communities. Arguably, psychodynamic theory and cognitive behavioral theory and the practices based on them are two of the most frequently used theories in the mental health field.[10] We both have different colleagues who practice either one of these theories (or a mixture of both), and we know that these two theories most certainly can be practiced in a sex-positive, social-justice-focused, trauma-informed manner. However, because of the dominance of these theories and without the humanizing influence of theorists, advocates, researchers, and organizers from historically excluded populations, many modern practitioners have used these theories to justify and/or perpetuate inaccurate and damaging understandings about people. As we reviewed in chapter 3, sex workers are not protected from, and are particularly vulnerable to, distorted understandings of them and their work. Too many practitioners have constructed profoundly untrue "information" about people's reasons for entering the industry, staying in the industry, and their need for therapy. Although no one theoretical orientation of psychotherapy is the sole progenitor of the oppressive paradigm, we assert that due to the underlying assumptions within the mental health field and the massive influence of psychodynamic, gestalt, and cognitive behavioral theories on the mental health field, they continue to be an element in influencing and maintaining the oppressive paradigm. Unchecked, these theories are a conduit for transferring the oppressive paradigm directly into the intimate space contained within a clinical session.

We urge you to remember (or to learn) the history of the theory that you use to conceptualize your clients. Take some time to read as much as you can of the source material of your preferred theoretical orientation. Further, do not just focus on how *you* understand and practice the theory that you use, and don't pretend that your theory does not have a history rooted in oppression. Examples of such oppression include Eurocentric solipsism, racist/gendered dismissals, and lack of inclusion in the theory, writing, or research development in psychodynamic theory, cognitive behavioral theory, and gestalt theory. The ethnic studies scholar Manning Marable,[11] in a broader framework, encouraged people to challenge ahistoricism by openly identifying patterns of systemic erasure of history, particularly when the history of psychology in the United States still involves oppression against marginalized communities. When applied to a therapeutic context, the lack of historical acknowledgment of a psychological theory results in some clinicians having the privilege of not understanding how historical inequities greatly contributed to present-day theoretical understandings of therapy.[12, 13] When you apply a theoretical orientation to the provision of health care services, we urge you to respond to Marable's call to be curious about the ways in which any given theoretical orientation has historically harmed the communities that your clients are from. Ask yourself, *"Why do I connect with the theory? What might some of this theory's historical harms be?"* When considering its use in your case conceptualization with a client who is a sex worker, ask yourself, *"What forms of erotophobia does my theory of choice espouse or have embedded in it?"* Instead of you pretending that the erotophobia is not there, we invite you to grapple with the theory. If there are problematic historical underpinnings of your theory rooted in erotophobia and whorephobia, we advise that you remake and adapt the theory as suits the clinical needs of your client . . . and be open about your adaptation. Name the historical problems in conversations, on your website, and (as appropriate) with clients in your clinical process. When you can, name and speak about those problems in groups of colleagues. When thinking about the theory to use in your work, remember that there is no perfect theory.

Just like the systems and institutions of which we are all a part, theories we use in therapy were mixed and baked in a history of racism, ableism, erotophobia, whorephobia, and other "isms," too. These are theories that we need to continuously adapt and change and, if the theory cannot be adapted and it does not serve people, we urge you to consider other theories. Mental health provision is an ever-evolving art and science. It is important and even necessary to move beyond theories that do not support us doing our best work or that undermine our client's well-being.

When discussing theories of sex-work-positive therapy, both of us are often asked, *"Which theories are the best for conceptualizing treatment of sex workers?"* We often playfully respond, "Worry about making the cake, not the icing." That is, getting into a competition about theories or knowing esoteric facts about them is not our main concern—for us, it's about creating understandings and processes to support a decrease in work-related stress and an increase in the agency and resilience of our clients. And though we will discuss some specific theories in the next section, to us, the question is always and ultimately *"What clinical practices are an expression of my underlying core values of people's right to dignity, respect, and the affirmation of their humanity?"* As such, we encourage your formation of a case conceptualization to move from titles of theories or labels of theoretical orientations to frameworks, principles, values, and lenses that are important to consider when working with sex-worker clients.

Hear us: We are not anti-theoretical. We believe that many theories most certainly have degrees of use and merit. However, instead of wondering which theory "works best" or which theory is "the best known" or "the latest thing" or the "most evidence-based" to use with clients who are sex workers, we share about and implement the practices that support a model of common factors, or critical pieces, that predict the success of the mental health process.[14, 15, 16] Although researchers have different opinions about the strength of these factors, our experience has supported the conclusion that the presence of a strong clinical relationship, a client's belief that therapy can be helpful or successful, and trust between therapist and client(s) are the essential components that will assist the client and the clinician toward a successful outcome. Trust feels particularly relevant because, as we noted in chapter 3, the oppressive paradigm has resulted in clinicians *of many different theoretical orientations* problematizing sex workers and stating that sex workers have mental health symptoms and concerns when they do not. Such processes have resulted in appropriate mistrust (or what we referred to as "adaptive suspicion" earlier) . . . and with good reason. In particular, trust is not just "Don't say something false." Trust can also be broken through the act of omission or passivity.

We encourage you to reflect on these factors as you think about tenets of the theories that you use in therapy, such as whether you focus your clinical work on a client's past or their present; whether you focus on a client's thoughts or their emotions (or a combination of both); whether you assign homework, or all the work is done in session; whether you work with individuals, partners in intimate relationships, families, or groups; whether the person most responsible for change is the client, the therapist, or some combination of the two. However you work, most importantly, are you thinking about the humanity of the person to whom you are providing services?

We hope that this chapter has begun to help you think a little bit about the theory that you use in your work with clients. No matter what your theoretical orientation, we are confident that if you are using the appropriate lenses of ethics and advocacy, you will be prepared to engage in mental health work that will be helpful for your client and sustainable for you. Further, as you co-create a relationship that is built on trust and mutual respect, you and your client(s) will engage in a mental health practice that has a positive and profound impact and that is one of the ways we shift culture.

Supporting Theories in Practice with Sex Workers

....

Based on their clinical supervision, Sylvia supports Malik to create a case conceptualization for his work with Arianne. With the theories of social justice and advocacy in place, Malik begins to wonder if and how Arianne's disempowerment from her professional work, her academic life, and her previous relationship may be linked to some of her nightmares and sleeping difficulties. Sylvia also assists Malik in applying a lens of intersectionality to gain perspective on how the people who work in the systems Arianne must interact with perceive her and how that may be causing additional stress and experiences of stigma for Arianne. These various theories provide Malik with a variety of questions that he can use to gain a more in-depth perspective on what is happening in Arianne's life while also finding ways to ask those questions with respect so that he can build rapport with this client. With these primary ideas in place, Sylvia, who is primarily a cognitive behavioral therapist, asks Malik what other theories he might want to use as he begins to create a structure for his upcoming sessions with Arianne. Malik and Sylvia speak about how cognitive behavioral theory combined with theories of intersectionality and social justice are helpful, but might not be fully sufficient to provide Malik and Arianne the support that they need in their work together. Sylvia suggests also reviewing tenets of trauma-informed practice, which may also allow Malik to see if and how experiences of violence and harassment may have created additional stressors for Arianne. Malik has learned a bit about trauma-informed practice, but is excited to learn more. During Malik's next session with Arianne, he checks in with her about what she has shared with him and how he is thinking of proceeding in their work together: "As I think about our last session, I am beginning to put some pieces together and want to check out some of these connections with you now. Is that okay with you?"

....

In addition to the noted theories that may harm sex workers in clinical practice if not reviewed thoroughly, we also believe that there are some theories that are helpful because they can be integrated with many different theoretical orientations very easily. Whether a brief-focused, cognitive behavioral therapist or a psychoanalyst, whether a relational gestalt therapist or an existential-feminist therapist (and everything in between), many clinicians working with individuals in the sex industry whom we have met have told us that there are three key theories that they integrate with their work: resilience, minority stress, and trauma-informed practice. Some clinicians have told us about one of these theories in their practice, whereas other clinicians have mentioned all three. Nevertheless, these three theories keep entering our conversations with trusted colleagues and mentors as they talk about their therapeutic practice with clients who work in the sex industry. These theories may not be the "main theory" that a clinician uses to conceptualize a client. Still, we present them here because it may be helpful for the clinician to add parts of these three theories to reinforce the dignity, respect, and humanity of the clients they serve.

Resilience. When working with themes related to sexuality and sex work in therapy, many scholars have noted that clinicians' sex positivity can be seen as helping a client to build *resilience,* or the human ability to adapt in the face of extreme psychological difficulty, trauma, adversity, or hardship, and cope with ongoing, significant life stressors.[17, 18] Other scholars have supported this definition of resilience, defining it as positive adaptation despite adversity.[19, 20] Such a theory of resilience seen through a lens of sex positivity results in the buffering of messages and biases that sex workers may encounter despite adverse reactions from the general public, from clients, or due to other workplace stress. Resilience can also aid sex workers in engaging in self-care (like taking a walk, engaging in fulfilling, intimate sexual play outside of work, maintaining an exercise routine, or cooking healthy meals, being able to actively disengage from work so that they can rest and relax) or other positive health-related behaviors (like connecting with social support, meeting new people, setting boundaries in relationships, and going to the doctor for physicals).

Such resilience can also take the form of sex workers adapting in the face of a variety of stressors, including discrimination from family and friends, physical danger, homelessness, violence, STI/STD risk, and police brutality.[21] When clinicians address such stressors, resilience becomes a paramount tool in learning about how individuals involved in the sex-work industry adapt to extremely harsh working conditions in order to stay safe. As resilience has a home within all disciplines of mental health practice, we strongly believe that a resilience-focused view of sex work may be particularly critical for clinicians. The clinician can ask questions to discover in what areas of their lives their clients have resilience (and in which areas of their lives that clinicians and their clients can co-construct more opportunities for resilience). Further, using sex positivity as a lens to engage with resilience and the strengths of sex workers to adapt to difficult working conditions is needed if clinicians want to work toward eradicating whorephobia and erotophobia.

Minority Stress. In addition to the theory of resilience, a second widely applied supplemental theory when working with sex workers is the theory of minority stress. In the early 2000s, Ilan Meyer[22] wrote a seminal article that applied theories of stress and coping to discrimination and stigma. Meyer's *minority stress* was a theoretical description of chronically high levels of stress faced by members of stigmatized minority groups such as people of color and LGBTQ+ people. Meyer described how stress may be caused by a number of factors, including lack of social support, lack of community, and lack of financial resources. Sound familiar? Yes, these factors are extremely relevant to clinical work with sex workers. Mental health scholars have built on Meyer's work to also describe how a stigmatized individual can also undergo such stress when that person experiences discrimination, the anticipation of rejection, hiding or concealing of an identity, or the internalization of the negative societal views. Currently, the minority stress theory is widely used in clinical practice, and is one that we often use in our practice with sex workers. Some of the best-understood causes of minority stress are interpersonal prejudice and discrimination.[23] The prejudice and discrimination that LGBTQ+ people experience, often on a daily basis, can take a toll on their mental and physical health.

For example, suppose Arianne from our vignette decides to tell her family that she is a sex worker. Her mother and father are not supportive and tell her that they are ashamed of her sex work. The minority stress model would suggest that Arianne is at greater risk of suffering physical or psychological symptoms due to the stress caused by coming out as a sex worker to her unsupportive family. Let us also suppose that, in addition to coming out to her family, the client in our vignette, Arianne, decides to tell one of her anthropology professors about her sex work. This professor warns her that she should not tell other people at the university due to possible discrimination in her department. Arianne might now be at even greater risk of psychological or physical illness because she faces stress from both school and family and has been shamed to not seek social support. The concept of minority stress is increasingly applied by mental health practitioners and public health officials who seek to understand and reduce minority health disparities.[24] As we noted in chapter 1, the concept of intersectionality can also impact minority stress, which creates added stress when specific sources of stress cross each other to create new sources of stress based on these intersections.

Trauma-Informed Practice. In addition to resilience and minority stress theories, the third theory that we often use in our work centers is trauma-informed practice. Although discussed through oral histories and in activist circles for decades, trauma-informed practice began to formally enter mental health literatures in the early 2000s[25] in reaction to the increased documentation of the traumatic impact of sociopolitical occurrences, such as community violence,[26] racial injustice,[27] and xenophobia related to immigration.[28] Although these experiences had been occurring for centuries, it was only during the late twentieth century that mental health disciplines began to more formally and comprehensively research, document, and create knowledge about the way that these experiences had a unique psychological impact through a lens of trauma and post-traumatic growth. Through a lens of trauma-informed practice, traumatic experiences are unique and also often result in shifts in cognitive schema, toward an understanding of the world as unsafe and unpredictable. Individuals processing such trauma also experience feelings of powerlessness and a reduction in self-efficacy.[29] Trauma-informed providers then focus on how trauma not only impedes everyday functioning but also results in lots of small, insidious shifts in our brains, hearts, and minds of which we are not even aware. Through a trauma-informed lens, providers focus on building resilience (yes, these three supplemental theories intersect a lot), decreasing the risk of subsequent traumatic experiences (if even possible), and initiating post-traumatic healing and growth. In trauma-informed mental health treatment, boundaries are clear, clients feel supported in defining their own concept of safety, and clinicians work to name moments of post-traumatic growth.

When hearing the words *trauma-informed,* you may have thought back to the oppressive paradigm that we outlined in chapter 3. The oppressive paradigm often results in clinicians believing that all sex workers have experienced trauma, or that traumatic experiences prior to sex work are the reasons that someone entered the field. Again, we want to be clear: Trauma-informed does not mean that we believe that all sex workers have survived trauma. In fact, trauma-informed might mean that dangerous work environments, police brutality, and sex workers' own violent clients may have been the precipitating factors of this trauma. *Trauma-informed does not mean trauma-focused or trauma-exclusive.* For us, trauma-informed means paying attention to trauma as a possible part of the equation.

Putting It Together

In this chapter, we hope you've begun to think of examining and re-creating your case conceptualization process. Specifically when working with sex workers, we hope that you have taken some elements of your own conceptualization out. And—like Malik and Sylvia—we also hope that there are parts that you add. Or—if you aren't adding anything—maybe you are naming certain theoretical lenses that you are using all the time and did not know how to put words to processes in which you were engaged.

Regardless of your theoretical orientation, we also hope that you reflected on your own ethics, your own positionality with respect to advocacy and social justice, and how these core tenets of practice with sex workers interact with your own theoretical orientation and case conceptualization process. Further, we trust that the introduction of our supplemental (but necessary) theories of resilience, minority stress, and trauma-informed care help you to think in increased detail about how you organize the information that clients provide in your sessions. We know that these conceptualization tools will provide you with more questions to ask and areas to explore with your clients in practice while simultaneously helping to generate a solid relationship of mutual respect and trust. Once the conceptualization is done, it's time to start planning and implementing interventions. Treatment planning can be an important next step for clinicians who will work with clients for a longer period of time, and having resources and ideas specific to sex workers can be vital to the success of your work. In our final chapter, let's look at interventions and treatment planning.

7

CLINICAL INTERVENTIONS AND CLINICAL PROCESS

....

Catarina Rivera is a thirty-one-year-old, queer-identified, Mexican American, cisgender female therapist who has been working at a large hospital in Columbus, Ohio. Catarina graduated from her doctoral program in clinical psychology approximately three years ago, and has been working in this hospital setting for the last year in the HIV prevention and treatment center (HPTC). In addition to its sexual health outreach programs, the HPTC has several psychotherapy programs that provide individual and group psychotherapy and psychiatric consultation to hospital patients in other departments and programs who need extra support. Dr. Rivera did her internship and postdoctoral fellowship in similar hospital settings throughout her doctoral training, and she has been excited to work with her new colleagues in developing a series of cultural competence trainings to various parts of the HPTC and in the hospital overall.

As she begins a new workweek, Dr. Rivera sees a new case on her caseload that has been transferred from one of her male colleagues: "Client was in my therapy group and asked for an individual therapist who was female, and you are the only one who had an opening on her schedule. Thank you!"

The patient, David, is a twenty-eight-year-old, Korean American, queer man who has recently been flagged by the hospital staff as needing some support after receiving sexual health testing services for three consecutive weekends as a patient in the hospital's emergency room. In his intake session with Dr. Rivera, David reports that his actual name is Hyun-Woo, but "I just say David because no doctor ever gets it right." Hyun-Woo notes that, for the past three weekends, he has been having some problems at a bar where he works. He reports that one of the bar's regular patrons has been soliciting him for sex after the bar closes. When he has gone to the patron's home, the patron usually has been intoxicated and demands that he have oral and anal sex with him without a condom. Hyun-Woo reports that the patron often "becomes belligerent when he's drunk," and that the man often offers him a lot of money, and "I feel like I can't say no." Hyun-Woo reports feeling "like a total wreck" when he leaves the patron's house early in the mornings after their encounters, exhibiting symptoms of dysregulation ("Sometimes, I'll be in the cab home and I can't stop shaking") and anxiety ("Every time I hear someone yell, I think about him"). When Dr. Rivera asks about Hyun-Woo's work at the bar and whether he has co-workers at his job in whom he can confide and can use as a safety system, Hyun-Woo reports that the bar is actually a strip club with a bar where he dances four nights per week. He reports that he lives in a studio apartment in the Brewery District, and that he often sends money to his sister, who is going to school in New York City. He reports that his parents are divorced and live in Seoul, and that "none of my family knows where I work."

Dr. Rivera has not worked with a client who is a sex worker before. As she gathers some initial assessment data, Dr. Rivera focuses on creating a strong rapport with her client. After her initial session with Hyun-Woo (Hyun-Woo's third session given that he is a transfer case), Dr. Rivera looks over the original therapist's intake and case conceptualization. She begins to think about a series of treatment goals and corresponding interventions with Hyun-Woo. Dr. Rivera asks herself, "How much should I focus on Hyun-Woo's work as a sex worker? Further, given that Hyun-Woo is a client in the HPTC, will focusing on sexual health be helpful?"

SO, YOU MAY BE wondering: *"But what should I do with all of this informa-tion when in a session with clients?"* That is, after examining your own biases and increasing your self-awareness (chapter 4), shifting your initial assess-ment and question processes (chapter 5), and diversifying some of the the-ories within your case conceptualization practices (chapter 6), you may now be wondering, *"What are the activities and interventions that I should use with clients?"* We would like to welcome you to our final chapter, or the "post–case conceptualization" part of the treatment process in mental health work.

As you have probably gathered by this point in the book, we feel that the clinician-client relationship is a key factor in the work that you do with cli-ents. Given the various harms endured by sex workers by a variety of social service and governmental entities, an appropriate level of mistrust from the client will enter the relationship with you. Your job is not to "erode" this mistrust, but rather to honor it and to create a space where sex workers can safely begin to examine trust with you. By "relationship," we mean foster-ing key conditions of warmth, empathy, openness, and genuineness while simultaneously creating a safe environment for discussion of sex work. As noted in the relationship between Dr. Rivera and Hyun-Woo in the vignette above, a focus on the rapport of the relationship can lead to sex workers' eventual disclosure of some of their own topics related to their work (in their own time) that they would like to bring into the therapy room.

By "relationship," we also mean that you as the clinician are bringing up issues of oppression, privilege, and marginalization that may exist in the room between you and a client (some that are visible, and some that are not visible), even when you identify with cultural privilege of various types. By "relationship," we also mean tending to feelings of discomfort experienced by your client about perhaps being in the sex industry (such as internalized whorephobia or erotophobia), and recognizing that "tending" might mean addressing it and gently challenging it when needed. However, "tending" can also mean recognizing that tending to other more key issues (such as trauma and safety) might need to be prioritized and that challenging of internalized stigma may need to wait until a future session or meeting. Thus, for us, the process of building rapport and building relationships with clients who are sex workers is continuous—trust is built; it is never a one-time event.

In addition, a needed intervention in any clinical relationship with a client in the sex industry is a continuous, explicit assessment of the elements that are inherent in a relationship where a power differential exists. In short: *It's not about you right now* (it can be about your stuff at another time in consultation or supervision). Given that your client is exposed to power at different ecological levels of systems all the time, it is vital that mental health services not be another place where sex workers feel depowered and shamed by one or more parts of their environment. Although there are increasing reports of sex workers who find their work a platform where they can flip gendered and racialized relations to power,[1] still other sex workers may leave a job or a day of work feeling demoralized and as though their power and agency have been taken from them. In these experiences, analyzing power dynamics in sex workers' lives can be a useful and helpful intervention. Thus, as you build this relationship, explicitly noticing the power dynamics within your relationships with clients can be crucial for clients in the sex industry to feel comfortable.

Treatment Planning

As you build a quality therapeutic relationship, you will begin to notice a time in your work when it is important to start working toward your treatment goals (if you have not started earlier in your work). Thus, a good mental health practitioner will work collaboratively with their client to construct a treatment plan that has achievable goals that provide the best chances of success in their mental health work. A mental health treatment plan is a set of written goals and objectives curated for the client to outline a plan of the clinician's work (and hopefully with the goal of eradicating or decreasing the client's symptoms, problems, or illness). A treatment plan will usually include the client's personal information, the diagnosis (or diagnoses, as is often the case with mental illness), a general outline of the treatment that the clinician will be utilizing, and space to measure outcomes as the client progresses through treatment. For those of us who work in settings where documentation is a critical part of practice, treatment plans are often driven by a client's symptoms (often called *symptom-based treatment plans*) or are driven by theory to generate more clinical relevance (called *theory-based treatment plans*).[2] Resource 7.1 is a sample treatment planning form that we often use in our practices to organize our goals for treatment and ensure that we are reflecting on and incorporating various parts of the client's life when deciding upon the treatment process.

> *And this is the part that really informed my practice is how policy could not override what was the sitting client presentation. [In my previous experience,] the policies that were in place to provide services, coun- seling, case management, therapy, were so wrapped up in respectabil- ity politics that they could not see my future [as a client], because they couldn't hear me or the future that I could see; they couldn't see my own client plan. They couldn't see the strengths that I brought.*
>
> —JASMINE

In our review of the effectiveness of a treatment plan, the most import- ant word is *collaboration.* When we think about our virtue ethics (return to chapter 6 for a review of this concept), a road map for someone else's growth must be done collaboratively with that person as an active contribu- tor. As is noted by our consultant Jasmine's comments above, we urge you to prioritize leveraging your client's agency as part of the treatment planning process. When you are constructing such a plan, what are the areas of their life or goals that are important to them? For example, if Hyun-Woo (from the vignette) was your client, would he want to focus on establishing a way to ban this client from his club? Does he want to focus on the symptoms of anxiety and fear that he feels? Although we may have ideas about where to start, building trust with clients who have been depowered by institutions of care means stepping aside and allowing them to take a leadership role in forecasting their own healing journey.

Part of collaborative treatment planning goes back to the awareness of our own biases (and naming our own needs to be important and our own whorephobia). Specifically, we all must balance what the client thinks is important with what we think is important to focus on in mental health treatment. Although we sometimes think so, we do not know better. We may have an expertise and can be aware of a client's certain behaviors (e.g., using different substances to cope with work-related stress), and pointing out those behaviors at the right time in the course of treatment can prove to be beneficial. However, pointing out behaviors as soon as we notice them and urging a client to focus on them could be more harmful than good (even if our aim is truly altruistic). For example, pointing out certain behaviors such as alcohol use as a coping mechanism can cause the client to feel shame and try to reduce such usage without establishing other, more positive health-related behaviors in its place.

When you are constructing such a treatment plan, we remind you that sex workers may be coming to therapy due to a multitude of worries and stressors. Some of these worries may have to do with their own feelings about sex work. Other stressors may center on other people's attitudes about their participation in sex work (even though the sex workers themselves may be perfectly fine!). As a result, clients in the sex industry whom we see may be stressed and could be stretched thin emotionally or psychologically from having to combat the whorephobia around them. Thus, a treatment plan should be constructed collaboratively, to help the client to thrive.

Tools in Your Toolbox

....

After consulting with a colleague with knowledge about clinical practice with clients who are sex workers, Dr. Rivera sits down with Hyun-Woo for their second meeting. She begins by explicitly noting that she has had the opportunity to reflect on their intake session. She explicitly notes that she is a sex-worker-positive therapist, and that she has been actively seeking education and training outside of their sessions to support Hyun-Woo. The two have an initial conversation about how much of their sessions may focus on connections between some of Hyun-Woo's symptoms and sex work. Dr. Rivera notes that she would like to ask a few questions about Hyun-Woo's work and its impact on his symptoms, but that she will not make any assumptions about possible connections between his symptoms and his work and will always check in to make sure she is understanding Hyun-Woo's experience correctly. Dr. Rivera also notes that Hyun-Woo does not have to answer any question that makes him uncomfortable, and that he can always ask Dr.

Rivera why she might be asking him a particular question or making particular suggestions for things to do inside or outside of session. Hyun-Woo agrees that this explicit check-in during their first few sessions will be helpful.

....

In addition, another way to help clients thrive is suggesting to the client to consider engaging in a variety of activities inside and outside of session to help them build their resilience and decrease symptoms of anxiety and shame (check in with the client to verify that they want to do so, of course). When you are completing Resource 7.1, it might be helpful to think about using one or more of the following seven key indicators as a treatment goal and/or an intervention to meet such a goal:

1. **Introduce short-term versus long-term treatment goals.** When you are initially planning mental health treatment, it will be important to explicitly determine what areas a client brings to us that need immediate attention and what areas might need more long-term work after the initial work is done. In our experience working with sex workers, we have often found that focusing on reduction of negative symptoms and addressing issues of safety can occur first in more short-term, action-oriented goals in the treatment plan. Such infrastructure in mental health work is critical, as clinicians need to triage and prioritize. Such triage can provide an initial reduction in symptoms and can result in initial improvement in functioning (more sleep, better mood, fewer symptoms of depression and anxiety, for example). These "small wins" in short-term goals can often instill hope that therapy will work, and will result in the client's participating even more intentionally in their treatment.

   Working on more short-term goals first may go against the way that you usually work (or may go against what the primary theory in your theoretical orientation would suggest should be your focus). For example, a clinician may want to immediately focus on more long-term, intrapsychic goals given some of the connections that the clinician has made when creating a case conceptualization. However, when a client needs stabilization, safety, and immediate support networks, the first stop on the therapeutic journey is clear. Also, when thinking about "long-term goals" with clients, be transparent about what medium- or long-term goals might look like so that clients who are sex workers (especially those who have not received mental health services before working with you) have a clearer road map of the therapeutic process.

2. **Assess for safety and safe working conditions for the client.** By this, we mean the safety that we infuse into the therapeutic rapport as well as the larger clinical relationship. We are also referring to the safety that the client has in various aspects of their personal and professional life. This one is so important, it's got its own section later in the chapter.

3. **Provide resources.** Some people have a lot of social capital and are plugged into a variety of resources (housing, legal services, shelters) that can be helpful to them, whereas others may not have connections to such services. We want to encourage you to increase your client's social capital. (If that sentence sounded like a treatment goal, we are succeeding. Increasing social support can be a goal for your client's treatment!)

In particular, we highly suggest three key resources that we use often. First, we suggest that you find a chapter of the Sex Workers Outreach Project (SWOP) near you to which you can refer your clients in the sex industry. Their website is fantastic (and it's a great resource for training and education for us and our colleagues, too!). Second, we also love the Cupcake Girls organization, whose mission is to provide support to those involved in the sex industry. This organization can also provide referral services, advocacy, outreach, and lots of nonjudgmental interface with individuals involved in the industry and can be a helpful tool for your clients. Third, we hope that you also consider linking your clients who are working online with Pineapple Support, a free support and therapy service for people working in the online adult industry. If you are providing individual services to a client, refer this client to a support group at Pineapple. If you are running a group and one member discloses their work in the industry, Pineapple may be helpful in finding that client a sex-worker-aware clinician who can provide them more comprehensive support. These three resources are ones that we use often, and they can be so helpful in linking our clients to the support that they need.

4. **Help to increase clients' ability to trust their own understandings and ability to adapt.** When applying the resilience and trauma-informed models from chapter 6, we can notice moments of resilience and strengths of sex workers' quick thinking and adaptability as they share themselves with us in mental health treatment. Encourage this by naming these moments as resilience in session, promoting opportunities for our clients' connection to their instincts, and supporting our clients in their ability to trust their judgment.

5. **Increase social support and create a village/wraparound approach.** You have probably recognized by this point in the book that one of the key experiences of some sex workers is isolation due to shame and stigma. However, numerous studies that we have read[3] and clients with whom we have worked have told us about the importance of having community in their life. So, we suggest helping clients find the support that they need. Such support can be professional (e.g., teaming up with another sex worker to provide simultaneous sexual services with one or more of their clients), but can also be joining a support or advocacy group, getting coffee with a friend, or joining a fitness or art class. Although the idea of social support has greater traction now, it cannot be understated. In addition, we recommend helping your clients in the sex industry create a wraparound approach. By "wraparound," we mean creating a small group of people in their lives who care about them and support them. These people can be other sex workers, employers or co-workers in a club or a sex-work-focused establishment, intimate partners, other care providers (such as doctors or massage therapists), friends, or family members.

As your client begins to create such a support pod, you may end up knowing people in that pod if you are providing services to a community of sex workers. Thus, with this wraparound, our ethical issue related to confidentiality that we discussed in chapter 6 comes up. We can't make the assumption that our client is out to anyone about their work. Therefore, asking clients about their desire to disclose information (even to other care providers) and honoring the client's current and anticipated relationship to outness about their work-related identities are crucial for positive mental health outcomes. Seems basic, right? Unfortunately, it is not—many scholars have noted that health care providers of various disciplines out their patients, clients, and/or consumers without their consent. In our experience, navigating confidentiality with different health care providers on a client's treatment team (e.g., psychiatrist, case manager, primary care physician, and others) can often result in such an unintentional outing. In addition, if you are coordinating with other care providers, make sure that your client knows about such coordinated care. It is always helpful to have an explicit conversation about what a client wants us to say and not say to those other providers, as the client may not be out about being in the sex-work industry to such a provider.

Lastly, a strong intervention that we use in session is to remind our clients in the sex industry of the importance for them to create their own support and social networks. Many clients without these networks may not know where to find these networks; we recommend several exercises in Lola Davina's workbook *Thriving in Sex Work*[4] that can help sex workers to know themselves and begin to identify appropriate networks. In addition to simply meeting people, we would encourage clients to leverage their networks to find ways to thrive and keep themselves safe (if you see hints of the resilience model from chapter 6 in this intervention, you are absolutely correct!). As clients build their resilience and increase their sense of agency both inside and outside of their work, you as the clinician may begin to see greater social confidence and more depth in their social relationships. Of course, some sex workers already have strong relationships and these dynamics may not apply; for others, such depth and increased social connection can be a signal that your client may be making positive progress toward meeting treatment goals.

6. Use a harm reduction model to cope with work-related stress.
When you are working with sex workers who experience acute and

large amounts of work-related stress, maladaptive coping (such as drugs and alcohol, self-harm, etc.) may begin to emerge as a way to navigate the stress of the job. A quick reminder that these behaviors were not the reason that our clients entered sex work, but that these behaviors often begin or sharply increase during a worker's tenure in the sex industry to cope with maladaptive and harsh work environments. We strongly urge you to think about addressing these coping strategies using a harm reduction model. Harm reduction incorporates a spectrum of strategies that include safer and managed use of drugs and alcohol (and abstinence if you and your client believe such a goal will be helpful and efficacious) and addressing conditions of use (along with the use itself). Originally stemming from G. Alan Marlatt's work focusing on drug abuse "meeting people who use drugs 'where they're at,'" harm reduction has become an integral intervention in many health care settings for a variety of behaviors related to disordered eating, self-harm, drug and alcohol abuse, and other negative health-related behaviors.[5]

Because harm reduction demands that interventions and policies designed to serve people who use drugs reflect specific individual and community needs, there is no universal definition of or formula for implementing harm reduction. What is important to remember is the need to consider how our clients who are sex workers are coping, will the coping have long-term harmful effects, and do we need to co-examine slight decreases in these harmful coping mechanisms along with increases in some other, more healthy coping mechanisms? Harm reduction can happen in one session or many sessions. Such harm reduction strategies can be a one-time, one-sentence verbal intervention or a calculated series of steps that you and your client work through over multiple meetings. However you integrate harm reduction, ensure that it is helpful for your client and that your client endorses that they want to reduce one or more negative coping strategies.

7. **Continue to focus on the therapeutic relationship.** As you work on your different goals and interventions, remember our words from chapter 5, chapter 6, and the beginning of this chapter: *The*

relationship with your client is critical. Maintain the therapeutic alliance. While processing different facets of your relationship, do not forget that if you make a mistake, you need to own it and repair it. Recognizing potential pitfalls and repairing inevitable ruptures are part of the work. Therapeutic ruptures happen in all kinds of mental health work—how we repair these ruptures indicates when and how people can trust us. Further, owning when you make a mistake is part of the process that a client will find humanizing (and, in some cases, may be corrective). As the advocacy theories that we discussed in chapter 6 are a key part of analyzing the power differential in mental health treatment, it is critical that this power differential is named and deconstructed when disagreements, ruptures, and/or mistakes happen. Further, it might be helpful for us to examine with our clients how our clinical relationship with them might be a conduit for future growth for them (and for us).

Regardless of which of these seven strategies you use (and maybe you use them all), we are confident that your implementation of these concerns will aid you in strengthening the relationship with your client and also help you to think about the clear road map that you will need to provide competent and comprehensive clinical care for your clients in the sex industry.

Assessing and Centering Safety Concerns

....

As Dr. Rivera and Hyun-Woo continue to develop their relationship, Dr. Rivera learns that Hyun-Woo feels safe while at work with his colleagues (many of whom are friends) at the club, but does not feel safe outside of the club due to the patron who has been increasingly aggressive. Dr. Rivera validates and normalizes Hyun-Woo's fears, and begins to gain insight that fear and anxiety are appropriate in this kind of situation. Dr. Rivera and Hyun-Woo speak in depth about Hyun-Woo's feelings regarding safety (as Dr. Rivera simultaneously assesses for safety). Hyun-Woo reports that his feelings of being unsafe occur primarily when he is alone, and he and Dr. Rivera begin to create a plan for people whom Hyun-Woo can call when he is by himself and begins to feel scared. Dr. Rivera also begins to work with Hyun-Woo to create a safety plan, with particular emphasis on other steps that Hyun-Woo can take both inside and outside of work. These steps include (1) speaking with one of the managers of the club about what is happening (Dr. Rivera and Hyun-Woo decide it might be helpful for the two of them to role-play this conversation in a future session) and (2) having co-workers who know about the problem on speed dial so that Hyun-Woo can call one of them if he becomes scared (either at his apartment or at the patron's house).

As the two continue to work together, Dr. Rivera continues to assess the quality of their clinical relationship. Hyun-Woo admits that he felt "disconnected" from the facilitator of his therapy group at HPTC and that many of the sex workers in the group felt as though "he compared his struggles as a marginalized person to ours. I know I felt unsafe, and I expect that others did, too." In exploring his relationship with clinicians, Hyun-Woo asks if he can call her Catarina to make the session a bit more egalitarian, and the two discuss the matter and decide that this switch in reference would make both of them more comfortable. In addition, Catarina advises that Hyun-Woo does not have to answer any question that makes him uncomfortable, and that he can continue to ask Catarina why she might be asking him a particular question or making particular suggestions for things to do inside or outside of session.

....

As we noted earlier, prioritizing safety for clients in the sex industry remains a needed and crucial intervention. In fact, an analysis of a variety of studies about sex workers' safety indicates that many providers do not assess safety for those clients whom they serve who are sex workers,[6, 7] in part because they have not received training to do so.[8] Given the variety of adverse working conditions that we discussed in chapter 2 (and some of the historical reasons that have led to such conditions discussed in chapter 3), to not acknowledge these safety concerns would be a disservice to clients. Further, we believe that such a lack of acknowledgment would also be an ethical issue.

What do we mean by safety? As you may be aware from your own engagement with different parts of the world, we mean *safety* to encompass lots of different kinds of behaviors, attitudes, and thoughts that allow an individual to be embodied without fear. Researchers have investigated psychological processes of safety within a mental health context, finding that feelings of safety have been correlated with interpersonal risk taking, feelings of connectedness, and wanting to take care of oneself.[9] Other scholars have noted that lack of safety is disproportionately found within minoritized groups, particularly those who have experienced systemic and cultural marginalization and oppression.[10] Through a lens of sex positivity, safety can also be interpreted to be a lens of sexual health in which individuals who feel safe may be more likely to set stronger boundaries within their work (this idea also directly intersects with theories of trauma-informed practice, as we discussed in chapter 6).

Many scholars and practitioners have theorized safety using a series of embedded circles, much like a dartboard. Adapting Urie Bronfenbrenner's model of ecological development[11] and with the individual at the center, the "circles model of safety" results in each circle representing a different level of context with which a clinician can co-create safety with their client.[12] Inner circles (circles closer to the center of the dartboard) indicate safety that is more individualistic and is within a more immediate context, such as housing, occupational support, intimacy, and establishing appropriate boundaries.

Although discussing and planning safety sounds like a needed intervention, we urge clinicians to implement such strategies with copious amounts of awareness and caution. Specifically, without acknowledging our own privilege in the room when discussing topics like safety, clients can feel invalidated and misunderstood by their mental health clinician. If you as a mental health clinician have not had experiences in the sex-work industry, do not assume that your experiences of safety are parallel to those of your client. In particular, if you have experienced a lack of safety due to harassment, violence, or discrimination because of a systemically oppressed identity, *we still urge you to not assume that your experiences of safety are parallel to those of your client.* Rather, we recommend that you navigate safety concerns within a frame of both you and your client gently exploring your client's experiences of perceived and actual safety. While you're facilitating both your and your client's growth, we urge you to integrate theories of resilience and advocacy (see chapter 6) when discussing safety, and use a "power-with" and not "power-over" frame of navigating these conversations. Specifically, help to empower your client by identifying steps that they can take to increase the client's safety, as done by Catarina and Hyun-Woo in the above vignette. In addition, linking clients to resources outside of your mental health environment (such as hotlines, support groups, neighborhood watches, shelters, sex-positive support groups, etc.) can also be helpful in creating such safety for clients.

A Few More Considerations

As you may have noted from our seven key indicators, there are many different roads to take in mental health work with clients who are sex workers. Safety is a key indicator that needs to be addressed due to the whorephobia and erotophobia that sex workers experience both inside and outside of their work environments. In addition to these seven indicators, we want to share a few more small tips that we have found helpful. These are tricks that we have learned along the way that have helped us; although they sound basic, it is often the most basic strategies that need repeating in our work.

Two core values that have served us individually and collectively when working with clients in the industry are *patience* and *adaptability*. Due to repeated discrimination and survival from harassment and violence, some clients who are sex workers may take longer to build trust, to take interpersonal risks with you, and to try interventions. Understandably so, many individuals are concerned about taking such steps, which need to be carefully monitored but not forced upon clients. Thus, adaptability enters the treatment process. Do not be afraid to adapt treatment plans, and do so explicitly with the consent of your clients. Adapting the treatment plan and normalizing that it is okay if a client has not met a certain goal by a certain time will continue to help a sex worker in your care to understand that the treatment is about that person and not about meeting a particular goal. Making room for the unexpected to happen is an important part of that adaptability, and may be difficult for clients who have experienced violence and connect to rigidity to find order and structure when other parts of their experience may seem chaotic.

Also, we encourage you to model; modeling is one way to increase sex workers' experiences of safety inside of mental health treatment. As clinicians, we should always be asking for consent and permission: when we switch topics, when we ask questions about intimate parts of the client's life, and when we ask about their experiences of work-induced trauma or violence. Simple questions like *"Are you okay if we talk more about [this other area]?"* are helpful in modeling what safety in relationships can look like with a provider.

Lastly, we want to say a word about terminating mental health treatment with individuals in the sex industry. As ending a treatment relationship with a provider can bring up a lot of things for anyone receiving mental health services, we want to encourage you to start the process of termination of treatment as early as possible in the ending phases of treatment. Given the mistrust that has formed between many sex workers and their care providers, a lack of ample time to process the ending of social services relationships may result in a sex worker believing that providers in the mental health industry who earn their trust will create trusting relationships and then abruptly end those relationships. Especially when sex workers may not have had a provider whom they could trust until their relationship with you, including lots of time to process the ending of the relationship can provide an experience in which your client can end a professional relationship with a mental health provider in a healthy way. We suggest starting the process at least a month in advance of your planned termination if you have been seeing the client for a long time, bringing up the topic of ending with increased emphasis as you get closer. For providers who work with clients for much shorter amounts of time, start termination with ample time relative to the amount of time that you have seen that client. If you are a provider who has seen a client only once, spend ten minutes talking about the fact that you may not see this person again, and what they might be taking with them from your relationship with them that they may want with a future mental health provider.

As you have read up to this point, interventions with clients in the sex industry stem not only from theoretical models of mental health practice, but also from core values of care and compassion, self-determination, and sex positivity that we have with clients. As you begin to create a road map for your work with a client who is also a sex worker, we urge you to keep our seven key indicators in your mind and pepper them throughout your work. We are sure that such an informed plan, combined with work that you have done on your own biases and attitudes as well as a solid theoretical case conceptualization, will result in positive treatment outcomes.

RESOURCE 7.1:
Adaptable Treatment Plan Template for
Clinical Work with Clients in the Sex Industry

Date: _____

Client #: _____

Clinician Name: _____

Date of Initial Assessment: _____

Number of Prior Sessions at the Time of This Treatment: _____

Session Frequency: _____

Expected Duration of Treatment: _____

Safety (including safety inside of work with clients):

_____

Is the client in crisis? ____Y ____N

If Yes, steps to stabilize client:

_____

_____

Are there referrals and/or other providers needed for consultation? ____Y ____N

If Yes, list any referrals needed or other providers with whom consultation is needed (with signed releases):

_____

_____

Seven Key Indicators

1. Introduce short-term versus long-term treatment goals.
2. Assess for safety and safe working conditions.
3. Provide resources.
4. Help to increase client's ability to trust their own understandings and ability to adapt.

5. Increase social support and create a village/wraparound approach.
6. Use a harm reduction model to cope with work-related stress.
7. Continue to focus on the therapeutic relationship.

Initial Phase of Treatment

1. Short-Term Goal #1:

   _____

   _____

   Intervention for ST Goal 1:

   _____

   _____

   Assessment of ST Goal 1 (Completed?):

   _____

   _____

2. Short-Term Goal #2:

   _____

   _____

   Intervention for ST Goal 2:

   _____

   _____

   Assessment of ST Goal 2 (Completed?):

   _____

   _____

Subsequent Phases of Treatment

3. Long-Term Goal #1:

_____

_____

Intervention for LT Goal 1:

_____

_____

Assessment of LT Goal 1 (Completed?):

_____

_____

4. Long-Term Goal #2:

_____

_____

Intervention for LT Goal 2:

_____

_____

Assessment of LT Goal 2 (Completed?):

_____

_____

Epilogue

HOPEFULLY BY NOW, AS we come to a stopping point in our learning about the unique needs of individuals who work in the sex industry, you are feeling more empowered to conduct various types of mental health practice with sex-work communities. We have reviewed numerous ways to reframe and shift our understanding of mental health work. In chapter 1, we defined sex work using a lens that incorporated privilege, power, and marginalization. Further, we located mental health work with sex workers within a context of oppression, sex positivity, resilience, and intersectionality in order to understand systems that work together to create large amounts of work-related stress for individuals in the industry. In chapter 2, we conducted an in-depth analysis about who sex workers are. Specifically, we analyzed sex workers through a lens of inaccurate media representations, resulting in a definition of the whorearchy and an in-depth analysis of social location and environment. In chapter 3, we provided a context of the mental health field's historical (and contemporary) attitudes and research biases. As we introduced and discussed the oppressive paradigm, we also noted how these biases infiltrate current understandings of sex workers' work environments, our understandings of why individuals enter the sex-work industry, and how to learn more about flawed and biased understandings of how sex workers experience trauma and traumatic stress.

In addition to reframing and shifting our understandings of mental health work with sex workers, we also reviewed numerous strategies of how a sex-positive, resilience model of clinical work can be used in mental health treatment with sex workers. In chapter 4, we discussed a variety of different ways to acknowledge our biases and different attitudes with respect to erotophobia and whorephobia. We discussed various strategies for mental health workers to engage in self-examination and understanding of their own positionality with respect to the practice of sex work. In chapter 5, we reviewed different phases of clinical assessment and the intake process. Considering a variety of factors, we identified different ways to decrease the stigma related to mental health practice and provided strategies to help provide an accurate depiction of what our clients in the sex industry bring into therapy. We moved to case conceptualization in chapter 6, discussing a variety of different considerations for appropriately using theories of personality and psychotherapy with clients who are sex workers. We also reviewed some current theories of therapy that are helpful in creating a sex-positive lens through which to approach future treatment. Finally, in chapter 7 we reviewed best practices in treatment planning for clients who are working in the sex industry. Using a variety of resources and a focus on safety, self-efficacy, and social supports, we reviewed different interventions for mental health workers to use in their work while providing ethical care to sex workers.

We also included several worksheets and templates for clinical documentation. We hope that these resources are useful to you, and we hope that you edit and customize them as needed to ensure that these resources work well with your practice. If you find certain changes, deletions, or additions helpful, we hope that you will let us and others know so that others can benefit from your increasing expertise. In addition, we hope that these resources are the beginning point for (or maybe an entry point into an already-existing set of) conversations about needed resources for mental health care with sex workers. Lists of resources, as well as templates for clinical intervention worksheets (for example, worksheets for safety plans, disclosing one's identity as a sex worker, etc.), are a needed set of documents in this work, and we urge you and your colleagues to make these lists and share them often.

Although these words are by no means an exhaustive list of how to make your practice more affirming of sex workers, we are confident that these strategies will put you on the right path. However, as we've noted multiple times throughout this book, one reevaluation of your practice is not enough to create a sex-worker-positive therapist. Continuous self-reflection on your work will be needed in order to continuously recommit to working with clients in the industry. Specifically, think broadly about the cycles and calendar of your work and recommit to checking in with your work. Finding regular times to self-assess your work and notice the presence and/or reduction of whorephobia, the presence and/or reduction of erotophobia, new best practices in clinical work, and other emerging trends will ensure that you are doing the work with all of the essential elements needed to continue to provide mental health services that celebrate sex workers and honor their resilience in erotophobic environments.

Now that we've taken you up to this point in your journey, it's time for us to say, "Until next time," and provide you with some additional considerations in your work toward making your practice more sex-worker-positive. For starters, we encourage you to publicize that you are sex-worker-friendly on your professional website, social media, and other public/front-facing marketing materials. Obviously, make sure you're ready for the response (do not just put these words in your marketing materials if you haven't done the work to be ready!). We know that you will be excited as new clients who are sex workers will schedule appointments and/or as colleagues will refer to you.

In addition, we hope that you couple this marketing with your continued exploration about sex-worker communities. By reading this text, you haven't completed a journey; rather, you have begun one. We want to frame the completion of this book as starting a long journey. With all of the supplies that you need alongside you, we hope that you will make many stops in your clinical work as well as seek out a lot of new opportunities to learn about, celebrate, and advocate for individuals and communities of sex workers. We encourage you to sign up for newsletters and/or follow sex-worker-led organizations, particularly those led by sex workers in your local communities from Black and various other communities of color. If you live in areas where there are no sex-worker-led organizations locally, social media will enable you to find other organizations that are close to you.

As you continue this journey, we also want to appreciate your vision for future steps and also invite you to be a change-maker. So much of what we share with you in this book both complicated what we learned in school (or what we learned in our training sites) and forced us to address the work that we do using new ways of understanding our relationship to mental health practice. It means a lot that you've hung in there with us throughout this text, in part because it means that there are many of us who want to do the work to correct the harm that has been done to sex workers by our professions. As you continue this journey, do not forget to create change so that, little by little, we can create the professions that we want for our clients and consumers. We hope that you will address the problematic language in your agency's initial assessment questions. We hope that you will say something if a colleague, supervisee, friend, or family member makes a whorephobic comment. And we hope that you will continue to let people know that you affirm sex workers in a variety of different ways, from the posts on your social media to the buttons on your bag.

We are excited that you are joining us in creating essential clinical care for sex workers. We know that we've asked you to do, and commit to, a lot, and we won't ask you to do things that we will not do. So, we commit to you that we (both individually and collaboratively) will continue to show up and make space for needed shifts and conversations about sex work and mental health, and we are excited to have you work with us. We hope to see you in various in-person and online spaces. Specifically, we will be excited to see you at political demonstrations, at professional conferences, and making space in communities (using virtual, in-person, and a combination of both platforms). If we can be of consultation to you, let us know. Thank you for committing to be the change.

Appendix: Resources

Internet-Based Resources

Peepshow: https://peepshowmagazine.com/2021/05/06/face-to-face-street
  -based-or-in-cyberspace-we-are-all-prostitutes
Sex Workers Outreach Project: https://swopusa.org
BIPOC Adult Industry Collective: www.bipoc-collective.org
Lysistrata: www.lysistratamccf.org
Sex Worker Self-Care Kit (Anna Borges, *Self*): www.self.com/story/sex
  -worker-self-care-kit

BLOGS

Mistress Jade Thunderstorm: https://www.neworleans-dominatrix.com/
Tits and Sass: https://titsandsass.com

PODCASTS

The Pornhub Podcast with Asa Akira: https://shor.by/phpod
Candy Girl Podcast: https://player.fm/series/candy-girl
Self-Help for Sex Workers (Lola Davina): https://podcasts.apple.com/us
  /podcast/self-help-for-sex-workers/id1265669183

Print and Article Resources

Davina, L. (2017). *Thriving in sex work: Heartfelt advice for staying sane in the
  sex industry*. Erotic as Power Press.
Dourado, I., Guimarães, M. D. C., Damacena, G. N., Magno, L., de Souza Júnior,
  P. R. B., & Szwarcwald, C. L. (2019). Sex work stigma and non-disclosure

to health care providers: Data from a large RDS study among FSW in Brazil. *BMC International Health and Human Rights, 19*(1), 1–8.

Press, E. (2021). *Dirty work: Essential jobs and the hidden toll of inequality in America.* Farrar, Straus and Giroux.

Sanders, T., Scoular, J., Campbell, R., Pitcher, J., & Cunningham, S. (2018). *Internet sex work: Beyond the gaze.* Springer International Publishing.

Treloar, C., Stardust, Z., Cama, E., & Kim, J. (2021). Rethinking the relationship between sex work, mental health and stigma: A qualitative study of sex workers in Australia. *Social Science & Medicine, 268,* 113468.

Notes

Chapter 1

1 Burnes, T. R., Rojas, E. M., Delgado, I. C., & Watkins, T. E. (2018). "Wear some thick socks if you walk in my shoes": Agency, resilience, and well-being in communities of North American sex workers. *Archives of Sexual Behavior, 14*(5), 1541–1550. https://doi.org/10.1007/s10508-016-0915-z

2 Burnes et al., "Wear some thick socks."

3 Sawicki, D. A., Meffert, B. N., Read, K., & Heinz, A. J. (2019). Culturally competent health care for sex workers: An examination of myths that stigmatize sex work and hinder access to care. *Sexual and Relationship Therapy, 34*(3), 355–371.

4 Press, E. (2021). *Dirty work: Essential jobs and the hidden toll of inequality in America.* Farrar, Straus and Giroux.

5 Treloar, C., Stardust, Z., Cama, E., & Kim, J. (2021). Rethinking the relationship between sex work, mental health and stigma: A qualitative study of sex workers in Australia. *Social Science & Medicine, 268,* 113468.

6 Sawicki et al., Culturally competent health care for sex workers.

7 Mac, J., & Smith, M. (2018). *Revolting prostitutes: The fight for sex workers' rights.* Verso Books.

8 Harcourt, C., Egger, S., & Donovan, B. (2005). Sex work and the law. *Sexual Health, 2*(3), 121–128. https://doi.org/10/1071/SH04042

9 Burnes et al., "Wear some thick socks."

10 Tomko, C., Nestadt, D. F., Rouhani, S., Silberzahn, B. E., Haney, K., Park, J. N., Galai, N., Logie, C. H., & Sherman, S. G. (2021). Confirmatory factor analysis and construct validity of the internalized sex work stigma scale

among a cohort of cisgender female sex workers in Baltimore, Maryland, United States. *The Journal of Sex Research, 58*(6), 713–723.

11 Bhopal, K. (2018). *White privilege: The myth of a post-racial society.* Policy Press.

12 Riemer, M., Reich, S. M., Evans, S. D., Nelson, G., & Prilleltensky, I. (2020). *Community psychology: In pursuit of liberation and well-being* (3rd ed.). Palgrave Macmillan.

13 DeCat, N., & Stardust, Z. (2020). Against inclusion: Sex work research, racial capitalism, and the knowledge industrial complex. In P. Liamputtong (Ed.), *Handbook of social inclusion: Research and practices in health and social sciences* (pp. 1–26). Springer Nature.

14 Riemer et al., *Community psychology,* p. 463.

15 deFur, K. (2020). Seven leadership skills for sexuality educators. In J. C. Wadley (Ed.), *Handbook of sexuality leadership inspiring community engagement, social empowerment, and transformational influence* (pp. 25–53). Routledge.

16 Bedi, S. (2015). Sexual racism: Intimacy as a matter of justice. *The Journal of Politics, 77*(4), 998–1011, p. 998.

17 Orne, J. (2017). Sexual racism. In *Boystown: Sex and community in Chicago* (pp. 62–78), p. 67. University of Chicago Press.

18 Jones, A. (2020). *Camming: Money, power, and pleasure in the sex work industry,* p. 993. New York University Press.

19 Riemer et al., *Community psychology.*

20 Davidson, L. J., & Kelly, D. (2020). Minding the gap: Bias, soft structures, and the double life of social norms. *Journal of Applied Philosophy, 37*(2), 190–210.

21 Darkwa, J. (2018). *Porn and the racial pay gap.* https://gal-dem.com/porn-racial-pay-gap/

22 Ohikuare, J. (2017). *The racist economics of interracial porn.* www.refinery29.com/en-gb/2017/07/167947/racism-pay-interracial-porn-industry-glamour

23 Jones, *Camming.*

24 Crenshaw, K. W. (1993). Demarginalizing the intersection of race and sex: A Black feminist critique of antidiscrimination doctrine, feminist

theory and antiracist politics. In D. K. Weisberg (Ed.), *Feminist legal theory: Foundations* (pp. 383–395). Temple University Press.

25 Crenshaw, K. W. (1994). Mapping the margins: Intersectionality, identity politics, and violence against women of color. In M. A. Fineman & R. Mykitiuk (Eds.), *The public nature of private violence* (pp. 93–118). Routledge.

26 Jones, *Camming*.

27 French, B. H., Lewis, J. A., Mosley, D. V., Adames, H. Y., Chavez-Dueñas, N. Y., Chen, G. A., & Neville, H. A. (2020). Toward a psychological framework of radical healing in communities of color. *The Counseling Psychologist, 48*(1), 14–46.

28 Burnes, T. R., & Chen, M. (2012). Multiple identities of transgender individuals: Incorporating a framework of intersectionality to gender crossing. In R. Josselson & M. Harway (Eds.), *Navigating multiple identities: Race, gender, culture, nationality, and roles* (pp. 113–127). Oxford University Press.

29 Burnes, T. R., Singh, A. A., & Witherspoon, R. G. A. (2017). Sex positivity and counseling psychology: An introduction to the major contribution. *The Counseling Psychologist, 45*(4), 504–527. https://doi .org/10.1177/0011000017710216

30 Mollen, D., Burnes, T. R., Abbott, D., & Lee, S. (2018). Sexuality training in counseling psychology. *Counselling Psychology Quarterly.* https:// doi.org/10.1080/09515070.2018.1553146

31 Abbott, D., Mollen, D., Anaya, E., Burnes, T. R., Jones, M., & Rukus, V. (2021). Providing sexuality training for psychologists: The role of predoctoral internship sites. *American Journal of Sexuality Education, 16*(2), 161–180.

32 Dawson, J., & Burnes, T. R. (2018). Sexuality and clinical supervision. In T. R. Burnes & J. E. Manese (Eds.), *Cases in multicultural supervision: New lenses, models, and applications.* Cognella Academic Publishing.

33 Hangen, F., & Rogge, R. D. (2022). Focusing the conceptualization of erotophilia and erotophobia on global attitudes toward sex: Development and validation of the sex positivity–negativity scale. *Archives of Sexual Behavior, 51,* 521–545.

34 Syme, M. L., Mona, L. R., & Cameron, R. P. (2013). Sexual health and well-being after cancer: Applying the sexual health model. *The Counseling Psychologist, 41*(2), 268–285.

35 World Health Organization. (2006). Defining sexual health: Report of a technical consultation on sexual health. Geneva, Switzerland: World Health Organization. www.who.int/reproductivehealth/topics/gender _rights/defining_sexual_health.pdf?ua=1

36 Ivanski, C., & Kohut, T. (2017). Exploring definitions of sex positivity through thematic analysis. *The Canadian Journal of Human Sexuality, 26*(3), 216–225.

37 Burnes et al., Sex positivity and counseling psychology.

38 World Health Organization, Defining sexual health.

39 Burnes, T. R., Peters-Long, S. L., & Schept, B. (2012). A resilience-based lens of sex work: Implications for professional psychologists. *Professional Psychology: Research and Practice, 43*(2), 137–144.

40 Weitzer, R. (2010). The mythology of prostitution: Advocacy research and public policy. *Sexuality Research and Social Policy, 7*(1), 15–29.

Chapter 2

1 Leigh, C. (1999). A first hand look at the San Francisco Task Force Report on prostitution. *Hastings Women's Law Journal, 10,* 59.

2 Leigh, A first hand look at the San Francisco Task Force Report.

3 Burnes et al., A resilience-based lens of sex work.

4 Sloan, L., & Wahab, S. (2000). Feminist voices on sex work: Implications for social work. *Affilia, 15*(4), 457–479.

5 Blasdell, R. (2015). *Reel or reality? The portrayal of prostitution in major motion pictures.* Unpublished doctoral dissertation, University of South Florida.

6 Brooks, S. (2021). Innocent White victims and fallen Black girls: Race, sex work, and the limits of anti–sex trafficking laws. *Signs: Journal of Women in Culture and Society, 46*(2), 513–521.

7   Buttram, M. E., Surratt, H. L., & Kurtz, S. P. (2014). Resilience and systemic risk factors among African-American female sex workers. *Psychology, Health & Medicine, 19*(4), 442–452.

8   Nuttbrock, L. (Ed.). (2018). *Transgender sex work and society.* Columbia University Press.

9   Glick, J. L., Theall, K. P., Andrinopoulos, K. M., & Kendall, C. (2018). The role of discrimination in care postponement among trans-feminine individuals in the US National Transgender Discrimination Survey. *LGBT Health, 5*(3), 171–179.

10 Butler, Y. (2021). Aligned: Sex workers' lessons for the gig economy. *Michigan Journal of Race & Law, 26*(2), 337–369.

11 Exner, J. E., Wylie, J., Leura, A., & Parrill, T. (1977). Some psychological characteristics of prostitutes. *Journal of Personality Assessment, 41*(5), 474–485. https://doi.org/10.1207/s15327752jpa4105_3

12 Surratt, H. L., Kurtz, S. P., Weaver, J. C., & Inciardi, J. A. (2005). The connections of mental health problems, violent life experiences, and the social milieu of the "stroll" with the HIV risk behaviors of female street sex workers. *Journal of Psychology and Human Sexuality, 17,* 23–44. https://doi.org/10.1300/J056v17n01_03

13 Exner et al., Some psychological characteristics.

14 Butler, Aligned.

15 Mysterious Witt. (2020). What is the whorearchy and why it's wrong. *An Injustice!* https://aninjusticemag.com/what-is-the-whorearchy-and-why-its-wrong-1efa654dcb22

16 Knox, B. (2014). Tearing down the whorearchy from the inside. *Jezebel.* Paragraph 4. https://jezebel.com/tearing-down-the-whorearchy-from-the-inside-1596459558

17 Smith, E. (2018). Sex work has a class problem. *Buzzfeed.* www.buzzfeednews.com/article/emilysmith/sex-work-class

18 McNeill, M. (2012). Whorearchy. *The Honest Courtesan.* https://maggiemcneill.com/2012/05/10/whorearchy/

19 Weitzer, R. (2012). *Legalizing prostitution: From illicit vice to unlawful business.* New York University Press.

20 Burnes et al., A resilience-based lens of sex work.

21 Feast, F. (2020). 5 sex workers talk about doing their jobs during COVID-19. *Buzzfeed.* www.buzzfeednews.com/article/fancyfeast/sex -work-from-home-stripping-bdsm-pandemic

22 Lam, E. (2020). Pandemic sex workers' resilience: COVID-19 crisis met with rapid responses by sex work communities. *International Social Work.* https://doi.org/10.1177/0020872820962202

23 Sawicki et al., Culturally competent health care for sex workers.

24 Campbell, R., Sanders, T., Scoular, J., Pitcher, J., & Cunningham, S. (2019). Risking safety and rights: Online sex work, crimes and "blended safety repertoires." *The British Journal of Sociology, 70*(4), 1539–1560.

25 Ślęzak, I. (2020). An ethnographic analysis of escort services in Poland: An interactionist approach. *Qualitative Sociology Review, 16*(4), 122–144.

26 Monk-Turner, E., & Turner, C. G. (2017). Thai massage and commercial sex work: A phenomenological study. *International Journal of Criminal Justice Sciences, 12*(1).

27 Davina, L. (2017). *Thriving in sex work: Heartfelt advice for staying sane in the sex industry.* Erotic as Power Press.

28 Burnes et al., "Wear some thick socks."

29 Lowthers, M. (2018). On institutionalized sexual economies: Employment sex, transactional sex, and sex work in Kenya's cut flower industry. *Signs: Journal of Women in Culture and Society, 43*(2), 449–472.

30 Davina, *Thriving in sex work.*

31 Bahri, J. (2019). Boyfriends, lovers, and "peeler pounders": Experiences of interpersonal violence and stigma in exotic dancers' romantic relationships. *Sexual and Relationship Therapy, 34*(3), 309–328.

32 Jones, *Camming.*

33 Sex Workers Outreach Project (SWOP) USA. (2017). National Transgender HIV Testing Day. https://swopusa.org/blog/2017/04/20/national -transgender-hiv-testing-day/

34 Underhill, K., Morrow, K. M., Colleran, C., Holcomb, R., Calabrese, S. K., Operario, D., Galárraga, O., & Mayer, K. H. (2015). A qualitative study of medical mistrust, perceived discrimination, and risk behavior disclosure to clinicians by U.S. male sex workers and other men who have sex with men: Implications for biomedical HIV prevention. *Journal of Urban Health, 92*(4), 667–686, p. 667. https://doi.org/10.1007/s11524-015-9961-4

35 Van Stapele, N., Nencel, L., & Sabelis, I. (2019). On tensions and oppor-
    tunities: Building partnerships between government and sex worker-led
    organizations in Kenya in the fight against HIV/AIDS. *Sexuality Research
    and Social Policy, 16*(2), 190–200.
36 Sawicki et al., Culturally competent health care for sex workers.
37 Lavoie, F., Thibodeau, C., Gagné, M. H., & Hébert, M. (2010). Buying
    and selling sex in Québec adolescents: A study of risk and protective
    factors. *Archives of Sexual Behavior, 39*(5), 1147–1160.
38 Mac, J. (2018). The laws that sex workers really want. In M. Adams, W. J.
    Blumenfield, D. C. J. Catalano, K. S. DeJong, H. W. Hackman, L. E. Hop-
    kins, B. J. Love, M. L. Peters, D. Shlasko, & X. Zúñiga (Eds.), *Readings
    for diversity and social justice* (4th ed.) (pp. 218–220). Routledge.
39 Van Stapele et al., On tensions and opportunities.
40 Mac, The laws that sex workers really want.
41 Mac, The laws that sex workers really want.
42 Mac, The laws that sex workers really want, p. 219.
43 Flanigan, J., & Watson, L. (2019). *Debating sex work*. Oxford University
    Press.
44 Mac, The laws that sex workers really want, p. 219.
45 Nevada Revised Statutes. *Chapter 201: Crimes against public decency and
    good morals*. www.leg.state.nv.us/nrs/nrs-201.html
46 Nevada Administrative Code. Chapter 441A.805: Use of latex or poly-
    urethane prophylactic required. www.leg.state.nv.us/nac/nac-441a
    .html#NAC441ASec805
47 Nevada Administrative Code. Chapter 441A.800: Testing of sex work-
    ers; prohibition of certain persons from employment as sex worker.
    www.leg.state.nv.us/nac/nac-441a.html#NAC441ASec800
48 Britannica ProCon. (2018). US federal and state prostitution laws
    and related punishments. https://prostitution.procon.org/us-federal
    -and-state-prostitution-laws-and-related-punishments/
49 Las Vegas Defense Group. (2021). Counties where prostitution is legal
    in Nevada. www.shouselaw.com/nv/blog/prostitution/counties-where
    -prostitution-is-legal-in-nevada/
50 Armstrong, L., & Abel, G. (Eds.). (2020). *Sex work and the New Zealand
    model: Decriminalisation and social change*. Policy Press.

51 Open Society Foundations/Sexual Health and Rights Project. (2012). *Laws and policies affecting sex work: A reference brief,* p. 5. www.opensociety foundations.org/uploads/f6ae725c-4344-47b1-bc32-abec41f791c3/sex -work-laws-policies-20120713.pdf

52 Mac, The laws that sex workers really want, p. 220.

53 US Congress, 116th Congress (2019–2020), S.3165—SESTA/FOSTA Examination of Secondary Effects for Sex Workers Study Act.

54 Van Ness, G. (2019). Hacking the hustle: Sex work, networks, and social reproduction under FOSTA-SESTA. In L. Bogers & L. Chiappini (Eds.), *The critical makers reader: (Un)learning technology* (pp. 245–257). Amsterdam University of Applied Sciences.

55 Jindal-Talib, A. (2021). *SESTA-FOSTA's impact on Black, LGBTQ+ sex workers' use of the internet and digital support tools.* Doctoral dissertation, University of Michigan.

56 Horn, T. (2018). How a new Senate bill will screw over sex workers. *Rolling Stone.* www.rollingstone.com/politics/politics-features/how-a -new-senate-bill-will-screw-over-sex-workers-205311/

57 Van Ness, Hacking the hustle.

58 Irwin, V. (2020). Some members of Congress want to study sex workers. *SF Weekly.* www.sfweekly.com/news/some-members-of-congress-want -to-study-sex-workers/

59 Merkley, J. (2020). Merkley, Sasse unveil urgently needed legislation to crack down on online sexual exploitation. www.merkley.senate.gov /news/press-releases/merkley-sasse-unveil-urgently-needed-legislation -to-crack-down-on-online-sexual-exploitation

Chapter 3

1 Gandy, P., & Deisher, R. (1970). Young male prostitutes: The physician's role in social rehabilitation. *JAMA, 212*(10), 1661–1666.

2 Benjamin, H., & Masters, R. (1964). *Prostitution and morality.* Julien Press.

3 Weatherall, A., & Priestley, A. (2001). A feminist discourse analysis of sex "work." *Feminism & Psychology, 11*(3), 323–340, p. 324. https://doi .org/10.1177/0959353501011003005

4 Sardana, S., Marcus, M., & Verdeli, H. (2016). Narratives of violence, pathology, and empowerment: Mental health needs assessment of home-based female sex workers in rural India. *Journal of Clinical Psychology, 72*(8), 827–838.

5 Weitzer, The mythology of prostitution.

6 Farley, M. (2004). Bad for the body, bad for the heart: Prostitution harms women even if legalized or decriminalized. *Violence Against Women, 11,* 950–964.

7 Farley, M., Baral, I., Kiremire, M., & Sizgin, U. (1998). Prostitution in five countries: Violence and post-traumatic stress disorder. *Feminism & Psychology, 8,* 405–426.

8 Weitzer, The mythology of prostitution, p. 10.

9 DeCat & Stardust, Against inclusion.

10 Burke, B. L., & Wrona, M. C. (2020). Mapping normality: Teaching abnormal psychology. *International Handbook of Psychology Learning and Teaching,* 1–25.

11 Burnes et al., A resilience-based lens of sex work.

12 Okoye, U. O., & Agwu, P. C. (2019). Why the high figures of sex-work migrants in Edo State, Nigeria? Considerations for social work practice. *Social Dialogue,* issue 20, 56.

13 Zamboni, B. D., & Zaid, S. J. (2017). Human sexuality education in marriage and family therapy graduate programs. *Journal of Marital and Family Therapy, 43*(4), 605–616.

14 Mosher, C. M. (2017). Historical perspectives of sex positivity: Contributing to a new paradigm within counseling psychology. *The Counseling Psychologist, 45*(4), 487–503.

15 Brown, T. W. (2019). *The myth of the oldest profession: Critiquing the archeological discourse of historic sex work.* Unpublished thesis, St. Mary's College of California.

16 Spanger, M., & Skilbrei, M. (Eds.). (2017). *Prostitution research in context: Methodology, representation, and power.* Routledge.

17 O'Neill, M. (2010). Cultural criminology and sex work: Resisting regulation through radical democracy and participatory action research (PAR). *Journal of Law and Society, 37*(1), 210–232. https://doi.org/10.1111/j.1467-6478.2010.00502.x

18 Weitzer, The mythology of prostitution, p. 20.

19 Orne, Sexual racism.

20 Comte, J. (2014). Decriminalization of sex work: Feminist discourses in light of research. *Sexuality & Culture, 18*(1), 196–217.

21 Gerassi, L., Edmond, T., & Nichols, A. (2017). Design strategies from sexual exploitation and sex work studies among women and girls: Methodological considerations in a hidden and vulnerable population. *Action Research, 15*(2), 161–176.

22 Minichiello, V., & Scott, J. (Eds.). (2014). *Male sex work and society.* Columbia University Press.

23 Davies, P., & Simpson, P. (1990). On male homosexual prostitution and HIV. In P. Aggleton, P. Davies, & G. Hart (Eds.), *AIDS: Individual, cultural, and policy dimensions* (pp. 103–119). Falmer Press.

24 Nuttbrock, *Transgender sex work and society.*

25 Weitzer, *Legalizing prostitution.*

26 Nuttbrock, L. A., & Hwahng, S. J. (2017). Ethnicity, sex work, and incident HIV/STI among transgender women in New York City: A three year prospective study. *AIDS and Behavior, 21*(12), 3328–3335.

27 Carpenter, B. (2000). *Re-thinking prostitution: Feminism, sex, and the self.* Peter Lang.

28 Cruz, K. (2018). Beyond liberalism: Marxist feminism, migrant sex work, and labour unfreedom. *Feminist Legal Studies, 26*(1), 65–92.

29 Marecek, J. (2001). Disorderly constructs: Feminist frameworks for clinical psychology. In R. K. Unger (Ed.), *Handbook of the psychology of women and gender* (pp. 303–316). Wiley.

30 Withers, J. (1975). Evaluating prostitution: The feminist dilemma. In J. James, J. Withers, M. Haft, S. Theiss, & M. Owen, *The politics of prostitution* (pp. 1–36). Social Research Associates.

31 Jones, *Camming.*

32 Hewer, R. M. (2021). *Sex-work, prostitution and policy: A feminist discourse analysis.* Springer Nature.

33 Carpenter, *Re-thinking prostitution.*

34 Kilbourne, J. (2000). *Can't buy my love: How advertising changes the way we think and feel.* Touchstone.

35 Minichiello & Scott, *Male sex work and society.*

36 Benjamin & Masters, *Prostitution and morality.*

37 Valera, R. J., Sawyer, R. G., & Schiraldi, G. R. (2001). Perceived health needs of inner-city street prostitutes: A preliminary study. *American Journal of Health Behavior, 25*(1), 50–59.

38 Erickson, P. G., Butters, J., McGillicuddy, P., & Hallgren, A. (2000). Crack and prostitution: Gender, myths, and experiences. *Journal of Drug Issues, 30,* 767–788.

39 San Francisco Women's Centers, Prostitution and Research Education Project. (1998). Stress disorder among prostitutes. *Off Our Backs, 28*(9), 6.

40 Rickard, W. (2001). "Been there, seen it, done it, I've got the t-shirt": British sex workers reflect on jobs, hopes, the future, and retirement. *Feminist Review, 67,* 111–132.

41 Thukral, J., & Ditmore, M. (2003). Revolving door: An analysis of street-based prostitution in New York City. Urban Justice Center.

42 Morse, E. V., Simon, P. M., Balson, P. M., & Osofsky, H. J. (1992). Sexual behavior patterns of customers of male street prostitutes. *Archives of Sexual Behavior, 21*(3), 347–357.

43 Weitzer, *Legalizing prostitution.*

44 Carpenter, *Re-thinking prostitution.*

45 Sawicki et al., Culturally competent health care for sex workers.

46 Minichiello & Scott, *Male sex work and society.*

47 Roberts, R., Jones, A., & Sanders, T. (2013). Students and sex work in the UK: Providers and purchasers. *Sex Education, 13*(3), 349–363.

48 Sagar, T., Jones, D., Symons, K., Tyrie, J., & Roberts, R. (2016). Student involvement in the UK sex industry: Motivations and experiences. *The British Journal of Sociology, 67*(4), 697–718.

49 Roberts et al., Students and sex work in the UK.

50 McClure, F. M., Chavez, D. V., Agars, M. D., Peacock, M. J., & Matosian, A. (2007). Resilience in sexually abused women: Risk and protective factors. *Journal of Family Violence, 23,* 81–88.

51 Burnes et al., "Wear some thick socks."

52 McIntosh, M. (1981). Who needs prostitutes? The ideology of male sexual needs. In C. Smart & B. Smart (Eds.), *Women, sexuality and social control* (pp. 53–64). Routledge and Kegan Paul.

53 Sagar et al., Student involvement in the UK sex industry.

54 Li, X., Wang, B., Fang, X., Zhao, R., Stanton, B., Hong, Y., Dong, B., Liu, W., Zhou, Y., Liang, S., & Yang, H. (2006). Grassroots participation, peer education, and HIV prevention by sex workers in South Africa. *American Journal of Public Health, 91*(12), 1978–1986.

55 Young, A. M., Boyd, C., & Hubbell, A. (2000). Prostitution, drug use, and coping with psychological distress. *Journal of Drug Issues, 30*(4), 789–800.

56 Surratt et al., The connections of mental health problems.

57 Jorjoran Shushtari, Z., Salimi, Y., Hosseini, S. A., Sajjadi, H., & Snijders, T. A. (2021). Determinants of safe sexual behavior of female sex workers in Tehran: The woman, her network, and the sexual partner. *BMC Public Health, 21*(1), 1–11.

58 Milner, A. N., Hearld, K. R., Abreau, N., Budhwani, H., Rodriguez-Lauzurique, R. M., & Paulino-Ramirez, R. (2019). Sex work, social support, and stigma: Experiences of transgender women in the Dominican Republic. *International Journal of Transgenderism, 20*(4), 403–412.

59 Logie, C. H., Wang, Y., Lacombe-Duncan, A., Jones, N., Ahmed, U., Levermore, K., Neil, A., Ellis, T., Bryan, N., Marshall, A., & Newman, P. A. (2017). Factors associated with sex work involvement among transgender women in Jamaica: A cross-sectional study. *Journal of the International AIDS Society, 20*(1), 21422.

60 Murphy, A. K., & Venkatesh, S. A. (2006). Vice careers: The changing contours of sex work in New York City. *Qualitative Sociology, 29,* 129–154.

61 Bolin, A., Whelehan, P., Vernon, M., & Antoine, K. (2021). Global aspects of sex and sexuality. In *Human Sexuality* (pp. 420–439). Routledge.

62 Weitzer, The mythology of prostitution.

63 Romans, S. E., Potter, K., Martin, J., & Herbison, P. (2001). The mental and physical health of female sex workers: A comparative study. *Australian and New Zealand Journal of Psychiatry, 35,* 75–80.

64 Ward, H., Mercer, C. H., Wellings, K., Fenton, K., Erens, B., Copas, A., & Johnson, A. M. (2005). Who pays for sex? An analysis of the increasing prevalence of female commercial sex contacts among men in Britain. *Sexually Transmitted Infections, 81,* 467–471. https://doi.org/10.1136/sti.2005.014985

65 Young et al., Prostitution, drug use, and coping with psychological distress.

66 Carstairs, C. (1998). Innocent addicts, dope fiends and nefarious traffickers: Illegal drug use in 1920s Canada. *Journal of Canadian Studies, 33,* 145–162.

67 Feucht, T. E. (1993). Prostitutes on crack cocaine: Addiction, utility, and marketplace economics. *Deviant Behavior: An Interdisciplinary Journal, 14,* 91–108.

68 Lasco, G. (2018). Call boys: Drug use and sex work among marginalized young men in a Philippine port community. *Contemporary Drug Problems, 45*(1), 33–46.

69 Young et al., Prostitution, drug use, and coping with psychological distress.

70 Krumrei-Mancuso, E. J. (2017). Sex work and mental health: A study of women in the Netherlands. *Archives of Sexual Behavior, 46*(6), 1843–1856.

71 Slim, M., Haddad, C., Sfeir, E., Rahme, C., Hallit, S., & Obeid, S. (2020). Factors influencing women's sex work in a Lebanese sample: Results of a case-control study. *BMC Women's Health, 20*(1), 1–9.

72 Willis, B., Vines, D., Bubar, S., & Suchard, M. R. (2016). The health of children whose mothers are trafficked or in sex work in the US: An exploratory study. *Vulnerable Children and Youth Studies, 11*(2), 127–135.

73 Tomko et al., Confirmatory factor analysis and construct validity.

74 Willis et al., The health of children whose mothers are trafficked.

75 San Francisco Women's Centers, Stress disorder among prostitutes.

76 MacLean, S. A., Lancaster, K. E., Lungu, T., Mmodzi, P., Hosseinipour, M. C., Pence, B. W., Gaynes, B. N., Hoffman, I. F., & Miller, W. C. (2018). Prevalence and correlates of probable depression and post-traumatic stress disorder among female sex workers in Lilongwe, Malawi. *International Journal of Mental Health and Addiction, 16*(1), 150–163.

77 Chudakov, B., Ilan, K., Belmaker, R. H., & Cwikel, J. (2002). The motivation and mental health of sex workers. *Journal of Sex & Marital Therapy, 28,* 305–315.

78 Silbert, M. H., & Pines, A. M. (1983). Early sexual exploitation as an influence in prostitution. *Social Work, 28*(4), 285–289.

79 San Francisco Women's Centers, Stress disorder among prostitutes.

80 San Francisco Women's Centers, Stress disorder among prostitutes.

81 Park, J. N., Decker, M. R., Bass, J. K., Galai, N., Tomko, C., Jain, K. M., Footer, K. H. A., & Sherman, S. G. (2021). Cumulative violence and PTSD symptom severity among urban street-based female sex workers. *Journal of Interpersonal Violence, 36*(21–22), 10383–10404.

82 Nabunya, P., Byansi, W., Damulira, C., Bahar, O. S., Mayo-Wilson, L. J., Tozan, Y., Kiyingi, J., Nabayinda, J., Braithwaite, R., Witte, S. S., & Ssewamala, F. M. (2021). Predictors of depressive symptoms and post traumatic stress disorder among women engaged in commercial sex work in southern Uganda. *Psychiatry Research, 298,* 113817.

83 Bowen, R., Hodsdon, R., Swindells, K., & Blake, C. (2021). Why report? Sex workers who use NUM opt out of sharing victimisation with police. *Sexuality Research and Social Policy, 18,* 885–896.

84 Cwikel, J., Chudakov, B., Paikin, M., Agmon, K., & Belmaker, R. H. (2004). Trafficked female sex workers awaiting deportation: Comparison with brothel workers. *Archives of Women's Mental Health, 7,* 243–249.

85 Fick, N. (2005). Coping with stigma, discrimination, and violence: Sex workers talk about their experiences. Sex Workers Education and Advocacy Taskforce (SWEAT). www.sweat.org.za/docs/coping.pdf

86 Sawicki et al., Culturally competent health care for sex workers.

87 Weitzer, The mythology of prostitution.

88 Burnes et al., A resilience-based lens of sex work.

89 Dong, W., Zhou, C., Rou, K. M., Wu, Z. Y., Chen, J., Scott, S. R., Jia, M.-H., Zhou, Y.-J., & Chen, X. (2019). A community-based comprehensive intervention to reduce syphilis infection among low-fee female sex workers in China: A matched-pair, community-based randomized study. *Infectious Diseases of Poverty, 8*(1), 97.

90 Kempadoo, K., Sanghera, J., & Pattanaik, B. (2015). *Trafficking and prostitution reconsidered: New perspectives on migration, sex work, and human rights.* Routledge.

91 Oliveira, E. (2019). The personal is political: A feminist reflection on a journey into participatory arts-based research with sex worker migrants in South Africa. *Gender & Development, 27*(3), 523–540.

Chapter 4

1 Pope, K. S., & Vetter, V. A. (1991). Prior therapist-patient sexual involvement among patients seen by psychologists. *Psychotherapy: Theory, Research, Practice, Training, 28*(3), 429.

2 Chen, I. Y., Szolovits, P., & Ghassemi, M. (2019). Can AI help reduce disparities in general medical and mental health care? *AMA Journal of Ethics, 21*(2), 167–179.

3 Burnes et al., "Wear some thick socks."

4 National Association of Social Workers. (2021). *Highlighted revisions to the Code of Ethics: 2021 highlights.* www.socialworkers.org/About/Ethics/Code-of-Ethics/Highlighted-Revisions-to-the-Code-of-Ethics

5 American Association for Marriage and Family Therapy. (2015). *Code of Ethics.* www.aamft.org/Legal_Ethics/Code_of_Ethics.aspx

6 American Counseling Association. (2014). *Code of Ethics.* www.counseling.org/resources/aca-code-of-ethics.pdf

7 American Psychological Association. (2017). *Ethical principles of psychologists and Code of Conduct.* www.apa.org/ethics/code

8 American Association of Sexuality Educators, Counselors, and Therapists. (2020). *Code of Conduct for AASECT certified members.* www.aasect.org/sites/default/files/documents/Code%20of%20Conduct-11.2020.pdf

9 Kottler, J. A., & Carlson, J. (2002). *Bad therapy: Master therapists share their worst failures.* Routledge.

10 Serani, D. (2019). *The ninth session.* Touchpoint Press.

11 Israel, T., Gorcheva, R., Burnes, T. R., & Walther, W. A. (2008). Helpful and unhelpful therapy experiences of LGBT clients. *Psychotherapy Research, 18*(3), 294–305.

12 Joy, E. E., & Bartholomew, T. T. (2021). Clients in context: Environment, class, race, and therapists' perceptions of generalized anxiety disorder. *Journal of Clinical Psychology, 77*(12), 2817–2831. https://doi.org/10.1002/jclp.23222

13 Crane, A. (2017). *Spent: A memoir.* Rare Bird Books.

14 Delacoste, F., & Alexander, F. (Eds.). (2008). *Sex work: Writings by women in the sex industry* (2nd ed.). Cleis Press.

15 Grant, M. M. (2014). *Playing the whore: The work of sex work.* Verso.

16 Minichiello & Scott, *Male sex work and society.*

17 Burgess, D. J., Beach, M. C., & Saha, S. (2017). Mindfulness practice: A promising approach to reducing the effects of clinician implicit bias on patients. *Patient Education and Counseling, 100*(2), 372–376.

18 Capers, Q., IV. (2020). How clinicians and educators can mitigate implicit bias in patient care and candidate selection in medical education. *ATS Scholar, 1*(3), 211–217.

19 Capers, How clinicians and educators can mitigate implicit bias, p. 211.

20 Bedi, Sexual racism.

21 American Association of Sexuality Educators, Counselors, and Therapists. (2022). Standards for Sexual Attitude Reassessment seminars. www.aasect.org/sites/default/files/2022%20Standards%20for%20SAR.pdf

22 Bedi, Sexual racism.

23 Stanley, J. L. Peer consultation groups in private practice: Ethical issues and cultural considerations. In T. R. Burnes & J. E. Manese (Eds.), *Cases in multicultural clinical supervision: Models, lenses, and applications* (pp. 147–160). Cognella Academic Publishing.

24 Burnes, T. R., & Manese, J. E. (Eds.). Introduction. In *Cases in multicultural clinical supervision: Models, lenses, and applications* (pp. 1–12). Cognella Academic Publishing.

25 Alexander, A. A., & Allo, H. (2021). Building a climate for advocacy training in professional psychology. *The Counseling Psychologist, 49*(7), 1070–1089. https://doi.org/10.1177/00110000211027973

Chapter 5

1 Jordan, C., & Franklin, C. (Eds.). (2020). *Clinical assessment for social workers: Quantitative and qualitative methods.* Oxford University Press.

2 Karson, M. (2017). There is no real therapy without assessment. *Psychology Today.* www.psychologytoday.com/us/blog/feeling-our-way/201708/there-is-no-real-therapy-without-assessment

3 Rasmussen, B. (2015). A psychodynamic perspective on assessment and formulation. In B. Probst (Ed.), *Critical thinking in clinical assessment and diagnosis* (pp. 151–169). Springer.

4 Wass, R., Harland, T., & Mercer, A. (2011). Scaffolding critical thinking in the zone of proximal development. *Higher Education Research & Development, 30*(3), 317–328.

5 American Psychiatric Association. (2022). *Diagnostic and statistical manual of mental disorders* (5th ed., text revision).

Chapter 6

1 Sperry, L., & Sperry, J. (2020). *Case conceptualization: Mastering this competency with ease and confidence* (2nd ed.). Core Competencies in Psychotherapy Series. Routledge.

2 Gehart, D. (2015). Treatment planning. In *Case documentation in counseling and psychotherapy: A theory-informed, competency-based approach* (pp. 95–109). Cengage.

3 Meara, N. M., Schmidt, L. D., & Day, J. D. (1996). Principles and virtues: A foundation for ethical decisions, policies, and character. *The Counseling Psychologist, 24*(1), 4–77.

4 Cheesmond, N. E., Davies, K., & Inder, K. J. (2019). Exploring the role of rurality and rural identity in mental health help-seeking behavior: A systematic qualitative review. *Journal of Rural Mental Health, 43*(1), 45–59.

5 Wampold, B. E., & Imel, Z. E. (2015). *The great psychotherapy debate: The evidence for what makes psychotherapy work* (2nd ed.). Routledge.

6 Alexander & Allo, Building a climate for advocacy training.

7 Burnes, T. R., & Singh, A. A. (2010). Integrating social justice into the practicum experience for psychologists: Starting earlier. *Journal of Training & Education in Professional Psychology, 4*(3), 153–162.

8 Burnes, T. R., & Manese, J. E. (2008). An analysis of social justice training in a predoctoral internship in professional psychology: Answering the call. *Journal of Training & Education in Professional Psychology, 2*(3), 176–181.

9 Lee, L. (2021). When she says women, she does not mean me. In N. West (Ed.), *We too: Essays on sex work and survival*. First Feminist Press.

10 Wampold, B. E. (2019). *The basics of psychotherapy: An introduction to theory and practice.* American Psychological Association.

11 Marable, M. (2015). *How capitalism underdeveloped Black America: Problems in race, political economy, and society.* Haymarket Press.

12 Bhopal, *White privilege.*

13 Stanley, J. L., Burnes, T. R., & Weinstock, J. S. (2017). Teaching the history of LGBTQ psychology. In T. R. Burnes & J. L. Stanley (Eds.), *Teaching LGBTQ psychology: Queering innovative pedagogy and practice* (pp. 39–60). American Psychological Association.

14 Browne, J., Cather, C., & Mueser, K. T. (2021). Common factors in psychotherapy. In T. Wykes (Ed.), *Oxford Research Encyclopedia of Psychology.* Oxford University Press.

15 Mulder, R., Murray, G., & Rucklidge, J. (2017). Common versus specific factors in psychotherapy: Opening the black box. *The Lancet Psychiatry, 4*(12), 953–962.

16 Wampold, B. E., & Ulvenes, P. G. (2019). Integration of common factors and specific ingredients. In J. C. Norcross & M. R. Goldfried (Eds.), *Handbook of psychotherapy integration* (pp. 69–87). Oxford University Press.

17 Burnes et al., "Wear some thick socks."

18 Dale, S. K., Cohen, M. H., Kelso, G. A., Cruise, R. C., Weber, K. M., Watson, C., Burke-Miller, J. K., & Brody, L. R. (2014). Resilience among women with HIV: Impact of silencing the self and socioeconomic factors. *Sex Roles, 70,* 221–231. https://doi.org/10.1007/s11199-014-0348-x

19 Grove, K. (2018). *Resilience.* Routledge.

20 Bonanno, G. A. (2012). Uses and abuses of the resilience construct: Loss, trauma, and health-related adversities. *Social Science & Medicine, 74,* 753–756. https://doi.org/10.1016/j.socscimed.2011.11.022

21 Rouhani, S., Decker, M. R., Tomko, C., Silberzahn, B., Allen, S. T., Park, J. N., Footer, K. H. A., & Sherman, S. G. (2021). Resilience among cisgender and transgender women in street-based sex work in Baltimore, Maryland. *Women's Health Issues, 31*(2), 148–156.

22 Meyer, I. H. (2003). Prejudice, social stress, and mental health in lesbian, gay, and bisexual populations: Conceptual issues and research evidence. *Psychological Bulletin, 129*(5), 674–697. https://doi.org/10.1037/0033-2909.129.5.674

23 Bailey, J. M. (2020). The minority stress model deserves reconsideration, not just extension. *Archives of Sexual Behavior, 49*(7), 2265–2268.

24 Shipherd, J. C., Berke, D., & Livingston, N. A. (2019). Trauma recovery in the transgender and gender diverse community: Extensions of the Minority Stress Model for treatment planning. *Cognitive and Behavioral Practice, 26*(4), 629–646.

25 Knight, C., & Borders, L. D. (Eds.). (2020). *Trauma-informed supervision: Core components and unique dynamics in varied practice contexts.* Routledge.

26 Cook, J. M., Simiola, V., Ellis, A. E., & Thompson, R. (2017). Training in trauma psychology: A national survey of doctoral graduate programs. *Training and Education in Professional Psychology, 11,* 108–114. https://doi.org/10.1037/tep0000150

27 Crosby, S. D. (2016). Trauma-informed approaches to juvenile justice: A critical race perspective. *Juvenile and Family Court Journal, 67*(1), 5–18.

28 Miller, K. K., Brown, C. R., Shramko, M., & Svetaz, M. V. (2019). Applying trauma-informed practices to the care of refugee and immigrant youth: 10 clinical pearls. *Children, 6*(8), 94.

29 Knight, C. (2018). Trauma-informed supervision: Historical antecedents, current practice, and future directions. *The Clinical Supervisor, 37*(1), 7–37, pp. 10–11. https://doi.org/10/1080/07325223.2017.1413607

Chapter 7

1 Berg, H. (2021). *Porn work: Sex, labor, and late capitalism.* University of North Carolina Press.

2 Gehart, Treatment planning.

3 Burnes et al., "Wear some thick socks."

4 Davina, *Thriving in sex work.*

5 Marlatt, G. A., & Donovan, D. M. (Eds.). (2005). *Relapse prevention: Maintenance strategies in the treatment of addictive behaviors.* Guilford Press.

6 Rekart, M. L. (2005). Sex-work harm reduction. *The Lancet, 366*(9503), 2123–2134.

7 McBride, B., Goldenberg, S. M., Murphy, A., Wu, S., Braschel, M., Krüsi, A., & Shannon, K. (2019). Third parties (venue owners, managers, security, etc.) and access to occupational health and safety among sex workers in a Canadian setting: 2010–2016. *American Journal of Public Health, 109*(5), 792–798.

8 Pederson, A. C., Stenersen, M. R., & Bridges, S. K. (2019). Toward affirming therapy: What sex workers want and need from mental health providers. *Journal of Humanistic Psychology,* 0022167819867767.

9 Mennicke, A., Geiger, E., & Brewster, M. (2020). Interpersonal violence prevention considerations for sexual minority college students: Lower campus connection, worse perceptions of institutional support, and more accurate understandings of sexual consent. *Journal of Family Violence, 35*(6), 589–601.

10 Booker, K. (2016). Connection and commitment: How sense of belonging and classroom community influence degree persistence for African American undergraduate women. *International Journal of Teaching and Learning in Higher Education, 28*(2), 218–229.

11 Bronfenbrenner, U. (1979). *The ecology of human development: Experiments by nature and design.* Harvard University Press.

12 Shelton, L. G. (2018). *The Bronfenbrenner primer: A guide to develecology.* Routledge.

About the Consultants

Sinnamon Love is a twenty-six-year veteran sex worker, community organizer, Black feminist pornographer, and an AVN awards and Urban X Awards Hall of Fame Inductee. In 2018 and 2020, Love served as a Fellow at the Sex Worker Giving Circle, the first-ever organization founded to put sex workers in a position of grantmaking to sex-worker-led organizations. She is the founder of the BIPOC Adult Industry Collective, an organization dedicated to bridging the wage gap in the legal sex trades through access to mental health resources, financial assistance, and peer-to-peer education. Love is a fierce advocate for Black Lives Matter, trans rights, sex-worker rights, and decriminalization of sex work and cannabis. Sinnamon identifies as kinky, bi, poly, and grown-up.

Twitter: @SinnamonLove
Instagram: @iamsinnamonlove
Website: www.SingleInBrooklyn.com
Interviews: sinnamon.love@gmail.com

Jasmine is a psychotherapist with a strong emphasis on intimacy post-injury/illness. She is the owner and lead therapist of Blue Pearl Therapy. Jasmine co-owns, with partner King Noire, award-winning Royal Fetish Films, and together they have more than twenty years of experience as adult entertainers, directors, and producers. The duo's love of the arts, film, and sex education is combined to produce erotica that stimulates and engages the audience to explore their sexual boundaries. Their work on the decolonization of sex and porn and politics has been featured in *Huffington Post, Rolling Stone, Paper* magazine, *VICE, Playboy, Forbes, Cosmopolitan,* BBC, *Psychology Today,* and more.

Twitter: @JetSetJasmine
Instagram: @JetSetJasmine
Website: www.JetSettingJasmine.com
iTunes: #RoyalFetishRadio

Vanessa Carlisle (she/they) earned their PhD in Creative Writing, Literature, and Gender Studies from the University of Southern California. They also hold a BA in psychology and an MFA in creative writing. Vanessa has worked in the sex industries for twenty-three years. Their novel *Take Me with You* (Running Wild Press) features a queer sex-working protagonist searching for her father, who has disappeared from LA's Skid Row. Vanessa's essay "How to Build a Hookers Army," about the peer-support and self-defense collective they co-founded, appears in the critically praised anthology *We Too: Essays on Sex Work and Survival* (Feminist Press), and their essay "Sex Work Is Star Shaped" appeared in the special issue of *South Atlantic Quarterly:* "Reading Sex Work."

Vanessa writes about and teaches a variety of sexuality-related topics, from sex workers' rights to polyamory, creating healthy boundaries, kinky skills, and more. They are a frequent guest lecturer, bringing both their lived experience and sharp critical analysis to classrooms and organizations on the cutting edge of sexuality studies. They also see individual clients who want to tap into their sexual expression and embodied wisdom to shift from stuck places.

In recent years, Vanessa has begun work in the field of death care, and is now a NEDA-Proficient death doula and guest instructor with the doula program Going with Grace. This work extends Vanessa's commitment to ending body-based stigma and smoothing the path for loved ones to experience greater connection while in the midst of big changes.

Twitter: @VCarlisle
Instagram: @VanessaCarlisle
Website: www.VanessaCarlisle.com

Angela McMahon (she/her) works in the nonprofit sector. Angela is passionate about utilizing her education and personal experience with homelessness and sex work to advocate for the unhoused community. Originally from Pittsburgh, Pennsylvania, she currently resides in Los Angeles, California, with her husband and two cats. Angela hopes to continue to use her voice to normalize and destigmatize conversations about sex work, inequity, and the whorearchy.

Index

goals *(continued)*

providing resources, 120–121

RESOURCE 7.1: Adaptable Treatment Plan Template for Clinical Work with Clients in the Sex Industry, 129–131

safety and safe working conditions, 120

short- vs. long-term, 119–120

using harm reduction models to cope with stress, 122–123

"Goldilocks approach" to sexual well-being, 11

H

harm reduction models, 122–123

health care discrimination, 28–29

health care workers' erotophobia, 66

hierarchy within communities of sex workers. *See* whorearchy

history

drug and alcohol use, 47–49

early labels of sex workers, 20

early mental health terminology, 38

feminists' critiques of sex work, 42–43

gendered notions of sex work, 43

importance of history of theory used to conceptualize clients, 103

media depictions of sex workers, 22

reasons for entering sex work: oppressive paradigm, 43–45

reasons for entering sex work: resilience/empowerment paradigm, 45–47

social science researchers, 38–42

trauma and post-traumatic stress, 49–52

HIV

high risk due to medical center discrimination, 28–29

legalization, and forced testing, 32

HIV prevention and treatment center (HPTC), 113

"hopeless" myth, 22

I

independent contractors, 25–26

independent sex-work contractors, 26

indirect vs direct sex work, 4

individualistic framing, 93

indoor sex work, 25

initial assessments, 74–76

building rapport with clients, 79–80

forms and paperwork, 80–82

intake interviews, 82

RESOURCE 5.1: Assessment Tool with Sex-Worker Clients, 90

writing assessment reports, 86–89

intake interviews, 82–86

intake reports, 86–89

internet

advantages of online sex work, 27–28

anonymous purchase of sex work, 38

examining sources of our attitudes, 60

gaps in labor protection, 28

impact of, 22

implications of location and environment on well-being, 28

OnlyFans, 28, 56, 92

Stop Internet Sexual Exploitation Act (SISEA), 34

Internet sex work: Beyond the gaze (Sanders, et al), 138

internet-based resources, 137

internships, 11

intersectionality, 9–10, 109

applying, 100, 106

SARs, 66

whorearchy, 25

interventions, 113–116, 119–123

adaptability, 127

focus on therapeutic relationship, 123–124

increasing clients' ability to trust themselves, 121

increasing social support, 121–122

modeling, 127–128

patience, 127

providing resources, 120–121

About the Authors

Dr. Theodore R. Burnes (he/him/his) is a licensed psychologist (PSY 25544) and a licensed professional clinical counselor (LPCC600) in the state of California. He received his MSEd in Psychological and Community Services from the University of Pennsylvania and his PhD in Counseling/Clinical/School Psychology from the University of California, Santa Barbara. He maintains a mental health practice in which he sees a range of clients and also supervises pre-licensed professionals, as well as creating space for voices of people working in the sex industry. Theo's practice as an educator has spanned a variety of mental health training programs at the master's and doctoral levels in professional counseling, clinical psychology, counseling psychology, teacher education, sex therapy, community psychology, and human resources management. He is currently a full professor of clinical education at the Rossier School of Education at the University of Southern California. Theo serves as a trainer for the Department of Mental Health for Los Angeles County in a variety of areas related to mental health practice. He has written numerous articles on training human service professionals to work with themes of sexuality and sex work in mental health work. Theo has a variety of professional interests that include the psychology of human sexual expression and sex positivity; teaching and training pedagogy in mental health services; clinical supervision; and social justice and advocacy. Theo is a fellow of the American Psychological Association, and is an associate editor for *Training and Education in Professional Psychology*. He is also a member of the board of directors for the California Association for Licensed Professional Clinical Counselors (CALPCC). His self-care activities include swimming laps, spending afternoons in the ocean, laughing with friends, and eating breakfast burritos.

Photo credit @Don Azu Keita

Jamila M. Dawson (she/her/hers) is a licensed marriage and family therapist (LMFT 97271) in the state of California. She received her MA in Clinical Psychology from the Chicago School of Professional Psychology, Los Angeles. Jamila's other publications include co-authorship of the book *With Pleasure: Managing Trauma Triggers for More Vibrant Sex and Relationships.* Her current professional areas of expertise include BDSM/kink, sex, ethical nonmonogamy, trauma, and relationships. In addition, Jamila has been a sex educator since 2005, providing pleasure-based sex-education classes and workshops at adult stores such as the Pleasure Chest and Babeland. She is the founder and owner of the psychotherapy practice Fire and Flow Therapy, and her work is grounded in interpersonal neurobiology, sex positivity, liberation psychology, and the politics of pleasure. She has been adjunct faculty at Antioch University Los Angeles and has lectured at the University of Southern California's School of Social Work. In addition, she has collaborated with BuzzFeed, AASECT Summer Institute, *MEL, Playboy, Harper's Bazaar,* and other media outlets. She has appeared on numerous podcasts, including *Girl Boner* and *Sex with Dr. Jess.* Jamila uses her Instagram and Facebook accounts to share practices, tools, and reflections on sexuality, racial justice, relationships, and mental health. She divides her time between Las Vegas and Los Angeles and can usually be found sitting in the sun reading old murder mysteries or new sci-fi.

About North Atlantic Books

North Atlantic Books (NAB) is an independent, nonprofit publisher committed to a bold exploration of the relationships between mind, body, spirit, and nature. Founded in 1974, NAB aims to nurture a holistic view of the arts, sciences, humanities, and healing. To make a donation or to learn more about our books, authors, events, and newsletter, please visit www.northatlanticbooks.com.